MW00608797

THE PRISON MEDITATIONS

OF

FATHER ALFRED DELP

With an Introduction by

THOMAS MERTON

Martino Fine Books
Eastford, CT
2021

Martino Fine Books
P.O. Box 913,
Eastford, CT 06242 USA

ISBN   978-1-68422-534-7

Copyright 2021
Martino Fine Books

Cover Design Tiziana Matarazzo

Printed in the United States of America On 100% Acid-Free Paper

THE PRISON MEDITATIONS

OF

FATHER ALFRED DELP

With an Introduction by

THOMAS MERTON

HERDER AND HERDER

1963

HERDER AND HERDER NEW YORK

232 Madison Avenue, New York 16, N. Y.

CONTENTS

INTRODUCTION

Those who are used to the normal run of spiritual books and meditations will have to adjust themselves, here, to a new and perhaps disturbing outlook. Written by a man literally in chains, condemned to be executed as a traitor to his country in time of war, these pages are completely free from the myopic platitudes, and the insensitive complacencies of routine piety. Set in the familiar framework of seasonal meditations on the Church year, these are new and often shocking insights into realities which we sometimes discuss academically but which are here experienced in their naked, uncompromising truth. These are the thoughts of a man who, caught in a well-laid trap of political lies, clung desperately to a truth that was revealed to him in solitude, helplessness, emptiness and desperation. Face to face with inescapable physical death, he reached out in anguish for the truth without which his spirit could not breathe and survive. The truth was granted him, and we share it in this book, awed by the realization that it was given him not for himself alone, but for us, who need it just as desperately, perhaps more desperately, than he did.

One of the most sobering aspects of this book is the conviction it imparts that we may one day be in the same desperate situation as the writer. Though we may perhaps still seem to be living in a world where, in spite of wars and rumors of wars, business goes on as usual, and Christianity is what it has always been, Fr Delp reminds us that somewhere in the last fifty years we have crossed a mysterious limit set by Providence and have entered a new era. We have, in some sense, passed a point of no return, and it is both useless and tragic to continue to live as if we were still in the nineteenth century. Whatever we may think of the new era, whether we imagine it as the millennium, the noosphere, or as the beginning of the end, there has been a violent disruption of society and a radical overthrow of that modern world which goes back to Charlemagne.

In this new era the social structures into which Christianity had fitted so comfortably and naturally, have all but collapsed. The secularist thought patterns which began to assert themselves in the Renaissance, and which assumed control at the French Revolution, have now so deeply affected and corrupted modern man that even where he preserves certain traditional beliefs, they tend to be emptied of their sacred inner reality, and to mask instead the common pseudo-spirituality or the outright nihilism of mass-man. The meditations of Father Delp were written not only in the face of his own death, but in the terrifying presence of this specter of a faceless being that was once the image of God, and toward which the Church nevertheless retains an unchanging responsibility.

The first pages were written in Advent of 1944, when the armies of the Third Reich launched their last, hopeless offensive in the Ardennes. Defeat was already certain. The Nazis alone refused to see it. Hitler was still receiving lucky answers from the stars. Fr Delp had long since refused to accept the collective delusion. In 1943 at the request of Count Von Moltke and with the permission of his religious Superiors, he had joined in the secret discussions of the 'Kreisau Circle', an anti-Nazi group that was planning a new social order to be built on Christian lines after the war. That was all. But since it implied a complete repudiation of the compulsive myths and preposterous fictions of Nazism, it constituted high treason. Since it implied that Germany might not win it was 'defeatism' — a crime worthy of death.

The trial itself was a show, staged by a specialist in such matters. It was handled with ruthless expertise and melodramatic arrogance before an obedient jury and public of SS men and Gestapo agents. The scenario did not provide for a serious defence of the prisoners. Such efforts as they made to protest their innocence were turned against them and only made matters worse. Count Von Moltke and Fr Delp were singled out as the chief villains, and in Delp's case the prosecution smeared not only the prisoner but the Jesuit Order and the Catholic Church as well. Moltke came under special censure because he had had the temerity to consult bishops and theologians with sinister 're-christianizing intentions'. The prosecution also tried to incriminate Moltke and Delp in the attempted assassination of Hitler the previous July, but this was obviously out of the question and the charge was dropped. This was plainly a religious trial. The crime was heresy against Nazism. As Fr Delp summed it up in his last letter: 'The actual reason for my condemnation was that I happened to be and chose to remain a Jesuit.'

Nearly twenty years have passed since Fr Delp was executed in the Plotzensee prison on February 2nd, 1945. During these twenty years the world has been supposedly 'at peace'. But in actual fact, the same chaotic, inexhaustible struggle of armed nations has continued in a different form. A new weaponry, unknown to Fr Delp, now guarantees that the next total war will be one of titanic destructiveness, when a single nuclear weapon contains more explosive force than all the bombs in World War II put together. In the atmosphere of violent tension that now prevails, there is no less cynicism, no less desperation, no less confusion than Fr Delp saw around him. Totalitarian fanaticisms have not disappeared from the face of the earth: on the contrary, armed with nuclear weapons, they threaten to possess it entirely. Fascism has not vanished: the state socialism of the Communist countries can justly be rated as a variety of fascism. In the democratic countries of the west, armed to the teeth in defense of freedom, fascism is not unknown. In France, a secret terrorist organization seeks power by intimidation, violence, torture, blackmail, murder. The principles of this organization of military men are explicitly fascist principles. Curiously enough, neo-Nazism recognizes its affinities with the French terrorists and proclaims its solidarity with them. Yet among the French crypto-fascists are many who appeal paradoxically to Christian principles, in justification of their ends!

What in fact is the position of Christians? It is ambiguous and confused. Though the Holy See has repeatedly affirmed the traditional classical ethic of social and international justice, and though these pronouncements are greeted with a certain amount of respectful interest, it is increasingly clear that their actual influence is often negligible. Christians themselves are confused and passive, looking this way and that for indications of what to do or think next. The dominating factor in the political life of the average Christian today is fear of Communism. But, as Fr Delp shows, the domination of fear completely distorts the true perspectives of Christianity and it may well happen that those whose religious activity reduces itself in the long run to a mere negation, will find that their faith has lost all content.

In effect, the temptation to negativism and irrationality, the urge to succumb to pure pragmatism and the massive use of power, is almost overwhelming in our day. Two huge blocs, each armed with a quasi-absolute, irresistible offensive force capable of totally annihilating the other, stand face to face. Each one insists that it is armed in defence of a better world, and for the salvation of mankind. But each tends more and more explicitly to assert that this end cannot be achieved until the enemy is wiped out.

A book like this forces us to stand back and reexamine these oversimplified claims. We are compelled to recall that in the Germany of Fr Delp's time, Christians were confronted with more or less the same kind of temptation. First there must be a war. After that a new and better world. This was nothing new. It was by now a familiar pattern, not only in Germany but in Russia, England, France, America and Japan.

Was there another choice? Is there another choice today? The western tradition of liberalism has always hoped to attain a more equable world order by peaceful collaboration among nations. This is also the doctrine of the Church. Fr Delp and Count Von Moltke hoped to build a new Germany on Christian principles. Pope John XXIII in his encyclical *Mater et Magistra* clarified and exposed these principles. If there remains a choice confronting man today, it is the crucial one between global destruction or global order. Those who imagine that in the nuclear age it may be possible to clear the way for a new order with nuclear weapons are even more deluded than the people who followed Hitler, and their error will be a thousand times more tragic, above all if they commit it in the hope of defending their religion.

Fr Delp had no hesitation in evaluating the choice of those who, in the name of religion, followed the Nazi government in its policy of conquest first and a new world later. He said:

'The most pious prayer can become a blasphemy if he who offers it tolerates or helps to further conditions which are fatal to mankind, which render him unacceptable to God, or weaken his spiritual, moral or religious sense.'

This certainly applies to cooperation with militant atheism first of all, but it applies equally well to any current equivalent of Nazism or militaristic Fascism.

ii

What did Fr Delp mean by 'conditions fatal to mankind?'

His prison meditations are a penetrating diagnosis of a devastated, gutted, faithless society in which man is rapidly losing his humanity because he has become practically incapable of belief. Man's only hope, in this wilderness which he has become, is to respond to his inner need for truth, with a struggle to recover his spiritual freedom. But this he is unable to do unless he first recovers his ability to hear the voice that cries to him in the wilderness: in other words, he must become aware of his devastated and desperate condition before it is too late. There is no question of the supreme urgency of this revival. For Fr Delp it seems clear that the time is running out.

In these pages we meet a stern, recurrent foreboding that the 'voice in the wilderness' is growing fainter and fainter, and that it will soon no longer be heard at all. The world may then sink into godless despair.

Yet the 'wilderness' of man's spirit is not yet totally hostile to all spiritual life. On the contrary, its silence is still a healing silence. He who tries to evade solitude and confrontation with the unknown God may eventually be destroyed in the meaningless chaotic atomized solitariness of mass society. But meanwhile it is still possible to face one's inner solitude and to recover mysterious sources of hope and strength. This is still possible. But fewer and fewer men are aware of the possibility. On the contrary: 'Our lives today have become godless to the point of complete vacuity.'

This is not a cliché of pulpit rhetoric. It is not a comforting slogan to remind the believer that he is right and that the unbeliever is wrong. It is a far more radical assertion, which questions even the faith of the faithful and the piety of the pious. Far from being comforting, this is an alarming declaration of almost Nietzschean scandalousness. 'Of all messages this is the most difficult to accept — *we find it hard to believe that the man of active faith no longer exists.*' An extreme statement, but he follows it with another: 'Modern man is not even *capable* of knowing God.' In order to understand these harsh assertions by Fr Delp we must remember they were written by a man in prison, surrounded by Nazi guards. When he speaks of 'modern man', he is in fact speaking of the Nazis or of their accomplices and counterparts. Fortunately not all modern men are Nazis. And even in reference to Nazis, when stated thus bluntly and out of context, these statements are still too extreme to be true.

They are not meant to be taken absolutely, for if they were simply true, there would be no hope left for anyone, and Fr Delp's message is in fact a message of hope. He believes that 'the great task in the education of present and future generations is to *restore man to a state of fitness for God*.' The Church's mission in the world today is a desperate one of helping create conditions in which man can return to himself, recover something of his lost humanity, as a necessary preparation for his ultimate return to God. But as he now is, alienated, void, internally dead, modern man has in effect no capacity for God.

Fr Delp is not saying that human nature is vitiated in its essence, that we have been abandoned by God or become radically incapable of grace. But the dishonesty and injustice of our world are such, Fr Delp believes, that we are blind to spiritual things even when we think we are seeing them: and indeed perhaps most blind when we are convinced that we see. 'Today's bondage,' he says, speaking of Germany in 1944, 'is the sign of our untruth and deception.'

The untruth of man, from which comes his faithlessness, is basically a matter of arrogance, or of fear. These two are only the two sides of one coin — attachment to material things for their own sake, love of wealth and power. Alienation results in the arrogance of those who have power or in the servility of the functionary who, unable to have wealth and power himself, participates in a power structure which employs him as a utensil. Modern man has surrendered himself to be used more and more as an instrument, as a means, and in consequence his spiritual creativity has dried up at its source. No longer alive with passionate convictions, but centered on his own empty and alienated self, man becomes destructive, negative, violent. He loses all insight, all compassion, and his instinctual life is cruelly perverse. Or else his soul, shocked into insensitivity by suffering and alienation, remains simply numb, inert and hopeless. In such varying conditions, man continues in 'blind conflict with reality' and hence his life is a repeated perpetration of a basic untruth. Either he still hopes in matter and in the power he acquires by its manipulation, and then his heart is one to which 'God himself cannot find access, it is so hedged around with insurance'. Or else, in abject self contempt, alienated man 'believes more in his own unworthiness than in the creative power of God'.

Both these conditions are characteristic of materialist man, but they also appear in a pseudo-Christian guise. This is particularly true of the negative, lachrymose and 'resigned' Christianity of those who manage to blend the cult of the status quo with a habit of verbalising on suffering and submission. For such as these, indifference to real evil has become a virtue, and preoccupation with petty or imaginary problems of piety substitutes for the creative unrest of the truly spiritual man. A few phrases about the Cross and a few formal practices of piety concord, in such religion, with a profound apathy, a bloodless lassitude, and perhaps an almost total incapacity to love. It is the indifference of a man who, having surrendered his humanity, imagines that he is therefore pleasing to God. Unfortunately Fr Delp suggests that such a one is already faithless, already prepared for any one of the modern pseudo religions, the worship of the Class, Race or State.

What can be done to save such resigned and negative Christians from becoming crypto-fascists? Certainly no amount of 'baroque glamorizing' of the mysteries of faith, no dramatic banalities, no false glitter of new apologetic techniques. Seen from the silence of Fr Delp's prison cell, the much publicized movements dedicated to so many worthy ends, take on a pitiable air of insignificance. Too often, he says, these efforts represent a failure to meet the genuine needs of man. Sometimes they do not imply even an elementary awareness of man's real desperation. Instead of being aimed at those whom the Church most needs to seek, these movements seem to him in many cases to concern themselves with the hunger of pious souls for their own satisfaction: they produce an illusion of holiness and a gratifying sense that one is accomplishing something.

Instead of the difficult exploratory and diagnostic work of seeking modern man in his spiritual wilderness with all its baffling problems, these movements are scarcely aware of anything new in the world — except new means of communication. For them, *our problems are still the same ones* the Church has been confronting and solving for two thousand years. It is assumed that we know what is wrong, and that all we lack is zeal and opportunity to fix it: then everything will be all right. It is not a question of truth or insight but of power and will, we imagine: all we need is the capacity to do what we already know. Hence we concentrate on ways and means of gaining influence so that we can obtain a hearing for our familiar answers and solutions. But in actual fact we are, with everybody else, in a new world, unexplored. It is as though we were already on the moon or on Saturn. The walking is not the same as it was on earth.

Too much religious action today, says Fr Delp, concentrates on the relatively minor problems of the religious minded minority and ignores the great issues which compromise the very survival of the human race. Man has gradually had the life of the spirit and the capacity for God crushed out of him by an inhuman way of life of which he is both the 'product and the slave'. Instead of striving to change these conditions, and to build an order in which man can gradually return to himself, regain his natural and supernatural health, and find room to grow and respond to God, we are rather busying ourselves with relatively insignificant details of ritual, organization, ecclesiastical bureaucracy, the niceties of law and ascetical psychology. Those who teach religion and preach the truths of faith to an unbelieving world are perhaps more concerned with proving themselves right than with really discovering and satisfying the spiritual hunger of those to whom they speak. Again, we are too ready to assume that we know, better than the unbeliever, what ails him. We take it for granted that the only answer he needs is contained in formulas so familiar to us that we utter them without thinking. We do not realize that he is listening not for words but for the evidence of thought and love behind the words. Yet if he is not instantly converted by our sermons we console ourselves with the thought that this is due to his fundamental perversity.

Fr Delp says: 'None of the contemporary religious movements take for their starting point the position of mankind as human beings . . . they do not help man in the depths of his need but merely skim the surface . . . They concentrate on the difficulties of the religious minded man who still has religious leanings. They do not succeed in coordinating the forms of religion with a state of existence that no longer accepts its values.' Before we can interest non-Christians in the problems of cult and of conduct that seem important and absorbing to us, we must first try to find out what they need, and perhaps also we might devote a little more thought to the question whether it is not possible that, in a dialogue with them, *they* might have something to give *us*. Indeed, if we do not approach the dialogue as a genuine dialogue, if it is simply a benign monologue in which they listen to us in abashed and grateful awe, we cannot give them the one thing they most need: the love which is our own deepest need also. 'Man,' says Father Delp, 'must be educated to resume his proper status of manhood, and religion must be taught intensively by truly religious teachers. The profession has fallen into disrepute and it will have to be reestablished.' What is needed, he says, is not simply good will and piety, but 'truly religious men *ready to cooperate in all efforts for the betterment of mankind and human order*'.

However these efforts must not be a matter of an interested and manipulative religious politic. The world has become disillusioned with religious politics devoid of genuine human and spiritual concern, interested only in preparing the way for preremptory doctrinal and moral demands. Fr Delp makes it clear that we are in no position to make such demands on modern man in his confusion and despair. The following paragraph is one of the most sobering and perhaps shocking in the book, but it contains profound truths for those who know how to listen:

'A Church that makes demands in the name of a peremptory God no longer carries weight in a world of changing values. The new generation is separated from the clear conclusions of traditional theology by a great mountain of boredom and disillusion thrown up by past experience. We have destroyed man's confidence in us by the way we live. We cannot expect two thousand years of history to be an unmixed blessing and recommendation. History can be a handicap too. But recently a man turning to the Church for enlightenment has all too often found only a tired man to receive him—a man who then had the dishonesty to hide his fatigue under pious words and fervent gestures. At some future date the honest historian will have some bitter things to say about the contribution of the Churches to the creation of the mass mind, of collectivism, dictatorships and so on.

More than this, Fr Delp realizes the profound responsibility of the Christian to his persecutors themselves 'lest those who are our executioners today may at some future time be our accusers for the suppression of truth'.

In such statements as these, Fr Delp makes no attempt to gloss over what he believes to be the truth, and he speaks with all the authority of a confessor of the faith who knows that he must not waste words. He himself adds, in all frankness: 'Whoever has fulfilled his duty of obedience has a right to cast a critical eye over the realities of the Church and where the Church fails the shortcomings should not be glossed over.' It is impossible to dismiss these criticisms as the words of an embittered rebel, disloyal to the Church. Fr Delp *died* for the Church. The words of one who has been obedient unto death cannot be dismissed or gainsaid. These meditations 'in face of death' have a sustained, formidable seriousness unequalled in any spiritual book of our time. This imposes upon us the duty to listen to what he has said with something of the same seriousness, the same humility and the same courage.

Nevertheless it must be recognized that since 1945 other voices have joined themselves to Fr Delp's and have reiterated the same criticisms. Perhaps they have done so in milder or more general terms, but there is a widespread recognition of the fact that the Church is seriously out of contact with modern man, and can in some sense be said to have failed in her duty to him. This awareness, though stated in general terms, can be discerned in statements of certain bishops, even of the Pope himself. Certainly the convocation of the Second Vatican Council was intended, in the mind of John XXIII, to meet precisely the situation which Fr Delp described with an almost brutal forthrightness.

Archbishop Hurley of Durban has recommended a radical reform in seminary education to enable priests to meet the new needs that confront the Church. Though stated with less urgency than the strictures of Fr Delp, these recommendations of the South African Archbishop reflect something of the same sense of crisis.

'Unless the change of methods is systematically pursued a first class crisis will result, for there is no better way of promoting a crisis than by allowing a situation to drift into change without adjusting the approach of those most directly involved in the situation. Priests engaged in the pastoral ministry are the persons most directly involved in the Church's day to day life and activity. There is therefore no more urgent task confronting us than a reconsideration of the methods by which our priests are trained for their ministry. If we fail to face up to it the developing crisis may strain to a breaking point the relations between a laity in desperate need of a new approach and to some extent led to expect it, and a clergy incapable of supplying the need.'
(Pastoral Emphasis in Seminary Studies, Maynooth, 1962).

iii

The diagnosis of our modern sickness has been given to us by Fr Delp in the most serious unambiguous terms. What of the prognosis?

First of all, he asks us to face the situation squarely, but warns that it is not enough to take a perverse pleasure in contemplating our own ruin. 'Pious horror at the state of the world will not help us in any way.' An apocalyptic mood of general disgust and contempt for the hopes of our struggling fellow-Christians would only further aggravate the negativism and despair which he has so lucidly pointed out to us. Yet at the same time there can be no question that we must start from where we are: we must begin with the fact that in the midst of a twisted and shattered humanity we too are leading an 'existence that has become a reproach'. Yet here he lays open to us the paradox on which our salvation depends: the truth that even in our blindness and apparent incapacity for God, God is still with us, and that an encounter with him is still possible. Indeed, it is our only hope.

Impatience, wilfulness, self-assertion, and arrogance will not help us. There is no use in Promethean self-dramatization. Things have gone too far for that. The encounter with God is not something we can produce at will. It is not something we can conjure up by some magic effort of psychological and spiritual force. Indeed, these are the temptations of the secular false prophets: the masters of autonomy, for whom 'untrammeled subjectivity is the ultimate secret of being', the artists of Faustian self-assertion whose efforts 'have silenced the messengers of God' and reduced the world to a spiritual waste land.

The Advent discovery which Fr Delp made, pacing up and down his cell in chains was that in the very midst of his desolation the messengers of God were present. This discovery was in no way due to his own spiritual efforts, his own will to believe, his own purity of heart. The 'blessed messages' were pure gifts from God, which could never have been anticipated, never foreseen, never planned by a human consciousness. Unaccountably, while he saw with a terrible and naked clarity the horror of his world gutted by bombs, he saw at the same time the meaning and the possibilities of man's condition. In the darkness of defeat and degradation, the seeds of light were being sown.

'What use are all the lessons learned through our suffering and misery if no bridge can be thrown from one side to the other shore? What is the point of our revulsion from error and fear if it brings no enlightenment and does not penetrate the darkness and dispel it? What use is it shuddering at the world's coldness which all the time grows more intense, if we cannot discover the grace to conjure up better conditions?'

In his Advent meditations, with all the simplicity of traditional Christian faith, and in images that are seldom remarkable for any special originality, Fr Delp proceeds to describe the ruin of Germany and of the Western world as an 'advent' in which the messengers of God are preparing for the future. But this golden future is not a foregone conclusion. It is not a certainty. It is an object of hope. But it is contingent upon the spiritual alertness of man. And man, as Fr Delp has already repeated so often, is totally sunk in darkness.

Man must begin by recognizing and accepting his desolation, in all its bitterness.

'Unless a man has been shocked to his depths at himself and the things he is capable of, as well as the failings of humanity as a whole, he cannot understand the full import of Advent.'

The tragedy of the concentration camps, of Eichmann and of countless others like him, is not only that such crimes were possible, but that the men involved could do what they did *without being in the least shocked and surprised at themselves*. Eichmann to the very last considered himself an obedient and God fearing man! It was this dehumanized bureaucratic conscientiousness that especially appalled Fr Delp: the absurd and monumental deception that practises the greatest evil with ritual solemnity as if it were somehow noble, intelligent, and important. The inhuman complacency that is *totally incapable* of seeing in itself either sin, or falsity, or absurdity, or even the slightest impropriety.

Two things then are necessary to man. Everything depends on these.

First he must accept without reserve the truth 'that life . . . by itself has neither purpose nor fulfilment. It is both powerless and futile within its own range of existence and also as a consequence of sin. To this must be added the rider that life demands both purpose and fulfilment.'

'Secondly it must be recognized that it is God's alliance with man, his being on our side, ranging himself with us, that corrects this state of meaningless futility. *It is necessary to be conscious of God's decision to enlarge the boundaries of his own supreme existence by condescending to share ours, for the overcoming of sin.*'

In other words, Fr Delp is reiterating the basic truth of Christian faith and Christian experience, St Paul's realization of the paradox of man's helplessness and God's grace, not as somehow opposed, fighting for primacy in man's life, but as a single existential unity — sinful man redeemed in Christ.

Acceptance does not guarantee a sudden illumination which dispels all darkness forever. On the contrary it means seeing life as a long journey in the wilderness, but a journey with an invisible Companion, toward a secure and promised fulfilment not for the individual believer alone but for the community of man to whom salvation has been promised in Jesus Christ. But as soon as these familiar words are uttered, we imagine that it is now once again a question of lulling ourselves to sleep in devout psychological peace. 'Everything will be all right. Reality is not as terrible as it seems.'

On the contrary, Fr Delp will have us turn back to the real contemporary world in all its shocking and inhuman destructiveness. We have no other option. This is the prime necessity. The urgent need for courage to face the truth of untruth, the cataclysmic presence of an apocalyptic lie that is at work not only in this or that nation, this or that class and party, this or that race, but in all of us, everywhere. 'These are not matters that can be postponed to suit our convenience. They call for immediate action because untruth is both dangerous and destructive. It has already rent our souls, destroyed our people, laid waste our land and our cities; it has already caused our generation to bleed to death.'

Yet at the same time, truth is hidden in the very heart of untruth. 'Our fate no matter how much it may be entwined with the inescapable logic of circumstance, is still nothing more than the way to God, the way the Lord has chosen for the ultimate consummation of his purpose.'

The light and truth which are hidden in the suffocating cloud of evil are not to be found only in a stoical and isolated individual here and there who has surmounted the horror of his fate. They must appear somehow in a renewal of our entire social order. 'Moments of grace both historical and personal are inevitably linked with an awakening and restoration of genuine order and truth.' This is most important. It situates the profound and mystical intuitions of Fr Delp in a securely objective frame of reference. His vision has meaning not for himself alone but for our society, our Church and for the human race.

In other words, Fr Delp prescribes not only acceptance of our 'fate' but much more, acceptance of a divinely appointed task in history. It is, note clearly, not simply the decision to accept one's personal salvation from the hands of God, in suffering and tribulation, but the decision to become *totally engaged in the historical task of the Mystical Body of Christ* for the redemption of man and his world.

It is then not only a question of accepting suffering, but much more, of accepting *happiness*. This in its turn implies much more than a stoical willingness to put up with the blows of fortune, even though they may be conceived as 'sent by God'. It means a total and complete *openness to God*. Such openness is impossible without a full reorientation of man's existence according to exact and objective order which God has placed in his creation and to which the Church bears infallible witness.

If we surrender completely to God, considered not only as an inscrutable and mysterious Guest within ourselves, but as the Creator and Ruler of the world, the Lord of history and the Conqueror of evil and of death, then we can recover the meaning of existence, we rediscover our sense of direction. 'We regain faith in our own dignity, our mission and our purpose in life precisely to the extent that we grasp the idea of our own life flowing forth within us from the mystery of God.'

Perfect openness, total receptivity, born of complete self-surrender, bring us into uninhibited contact with God. In finding him we find our true selves. We return to the true order he has willed for us.

Such texts show that Fr Delp was at the same time profoundly mystical and wide open to the broadest ideals of Christian humanism. It was by the gift of mystical intuition that he not only found himself in God but also situated himself perfectly in God's order and man's society, even though paradoxically his place was to be a condemned man in the prison of an unjust and absurd government. Yet it was here that, as this book so eloquently proves to us, he fulfilled all that God asked of him. It was here that he could write, without exaggeration, 'To restore divine order and to proclaim God's presence — these have been my vocation.'

Fr Delp's exact obedience to God, his perfect acceptance of God's order in the midst of disorder, was what gave him a sublime authority in denouncing the cowardice of Christians who seek refuge from reality in trifling concerns, petty sectarian opinions, futile ritualism or religious technicalities which they alone can understand. Christians must not be afraid to be people, and to enter into a genuine dialogue with other men, precisely perhaps with those men they most fear or stand most ready to condemn.

'The genuine dialogue no longer exists', says Fr Delp, 'because there are no genuine partners to engage in it. People are frightened. They are scared to stride out firmly and honestly to the boundaries of their potential powers because they are afraid of what they will find at the borderline.'

In his impassioned plea for Christian liberty and personal dignity, Fr Delp stands out as an advocate of true Christian humanism. This is exactly the opposite of the promethean pseudo-humanism of anti-Christian culture since the Renaissance.

The supposed 'creativity' claimed by the untrammeled subjectivism of men who seek complete autonomy defeats itself, because man centered on himself inevitably becomes destructive.

The humanism of Fr Delp, which is also the humanism of the Church, recognizes that man has to be rescued precisely from this spurious autonomy which can only ruin him. He must be liberated from fixation upon his own subjective needs and compulsions, and recognize that he cannot fully become himself until he knows his need for the world and his duty of serving it.

In bare outline, man's service of the world consists not in brandishing weapons to destroy other men and hostile societies, but in creating an order based on God's plan for his creation, beginning with minimum standard for a truly human existence for all men. Living space, law and order, nourishment for *all*, are basic needs without which there can be no peace and no stability on earth. 'No faith, no education, no government, no science, no art, no wisdom will help mankind if the unfailing certainty of the minimum is lacking.'

There is also an ethical minimum: honesty in every field, self respect and mutual respect for all men, human solidarity among all races and nations. There must finally be a 'minimum of transcendence', in other words the cultural and spiritual needs of man must be met. In the words of Pope John XXIII, in *Mater et Magistra*: 'Today the Church is confronted with *the immense task of giving a human and Christian note to modern civilization:* a note that is almost asked by that civilization itself for its further development *and even for its continued existence.*' It is no easy task to meet these minimal standards. At the present moment the fury and compulsions of the Cold War seem to be the chief obstacle to our progress. Yet we too are in the same 'advent' as Fr Delp, and its laws are the same for us. If we pay attention, rouse ourselves from our despairing sleep, open our hearts without reserve to the God who speaks to us in the very wilderness where we now are, we can begin the work he asks of us: the work of restoring order to society, and bringing peace to the world, so that eventually man may begin to be healed of his mortal sickness, and that one day a sane society may emerge from our present confusion.

Is this impossible? When Fr Delp died, he surrendered his life into the hands of God with the full conviction that it was not only possible, but that the work would one day be done.

But he also believed that the only hope for the world was this return to order and the emergence of the 'new man', who knows that 'adoration of God is the road that leads man to himself'.

Unless man is made new, in the new order for which Fr Delp laid down his life, there is no hope for our society, there is no hope for the human race. For man, in his present condition, has been reduced to helplessness. All his efforts to save himself by his own ingenuity are futile. They bring him closer and closer to his own destruction.

Such then is the deeply disturbing yet hopeful message of these pages. It is the message not of a politician, but of a mystic. Yet this mystic recognized his inescapable responsibility to be involved in politics. And because he followed messengers of God into the midst of a fanatical and absurd political crisis, he was put to death for his pains.

What remains now is to understand this final most important lesson. The place of the mystic and the prophet in the twentieth century is not totally outside of society, not utterly remote from the world. Spirituality, religion, mysticism are not an unequivocal rejection of the human race in order to seek one's own individual salvation without concern for the rest of men. Nor is true worship a matter of standing aside and praying for the world, without any concept of its problems and its desperation.

The mystic and the spiritual man who in our day remain indifferent to the problems of their fellow men, who are not fully capable of facing those problems, will find themselves inevitably involved in the same ruin. They will suffer the same deceptions, be implicated in the same crimes. They will go down to ruin with the same blindness and the same insensitivity to the presence of evil. They will be deaf to the voice crying in the wilderness, for they will have listened to some other, more comforting voice, of their own making. This is the penalty of evasion and complacency.

Even contemplative and cloistered religious, perhaps especially these, need to be attuned to the deepest problems of the contemporary world. This does not mean that they must leave their solitude and engage in the struggle and confusion in which they can only be less useful than they would be in their cloister. They must preserve their unique perspective, which solitude alone can give them, and from their vantage point they must understand the world's anguish and share it in their own way, which may, in fact, be very like the experience of Fr Delp.

No one has a more solemn obligation to understand the true nature of man's predicament than he who is called to a life of special holiness and dedication. The priest, the religious, the lay-leader must, whether he likes it or not, fulfil in the world the role of a prophet. If he does not face the anguish of being a true prophet, he must enjoy the carrion comfort of acceptance in the society of the deluded by becoming a false prophet and participating in their delusions.

Thomas Merton.
October 1962.

EXTRACTS FROM FR DELP'S DIARY

EXTRACTS FROM FR DELP'S DIARY

1944

December 28th

In the course of these last long weeks life has become suddenly much less rigid. A great deal that was once quite simple and ordinary seems to have taken on a new dimension. Things seem clearer and at the same time more profound; one sees all sorts of unexpected angles. And above all God has become almost tangible. Things I have always known and believed now seem so concrete; I believe them but I also live them.

For instance how I used to mouth the words 'hope' and 'trust'. I know now that I used them uncomprehending, like a child. And in doing so I deprived my life of much fruitfulness and achievement and I also cheated my fellow men of many substantial blessings because I was incapable of taking really seriously God's command that we should trust him absolutely and whole-heartedly. Only a man who really believes and hopes and trusts can form any idea of humanity's real status or catch a glimpse of the divine perspective.

December 29th

Far more than a civilisation or a rich heritage was lost when the universal order went the way of medieval and ancient civilisations. Western man today is spiritually homeless, naked and exposed. The moment he starts to be anything beyond 'one of the masses' he becomes terribly aware of that isolation which has always encompassed the great. He realises his homelessness and his exposure. So he sets to work to build himself some sort of house and shelter. Our ancestors, those among them who were really great men, could have left us a legacy much more helpful for our progress. We can only account for the contorted thought of men like Paracelsus or Bohme on the grounds that life's insufferable loneliness and lack of design forced them to build a shelter for themselves. And although it is such a self-willed and distorted and angular structure it still has the marks of painstaking care and trouble and in that must command our respect. Goethe had rather more success; his instinct was surer and it led him to guess at some of nature's more important designs. Moreover he had a good – though not in all respects dependable – master whose ideas he copied to a very large extent.

Every now and then someone comes along and tries to impose his own plan on the rest of the world, either because he knows he has stumbled on a universal need or because he thinks he has and over-estimates his own infallibility. Such men will never lack followers since so many people long for a well-founded communal home to which they can feel they 'belong'. Time after time in the end they come to realise that the shelter offered is not all it purports to be – it cannot keep out the wind and the weather. And time and time again the deluded seekers conclude they have been taken in by a mountebank; the man probably had no intention of deliberately deceiving but he was nevertheless a charlatan misleading himself and others.

*　　*　　*

It is quite remarkable. Since Midnight Mass on

Christmas Eve I have become almost light-heartedly confident although nothing outwardly has changed. Somewhere within me ice has been melted by the prayers for love and life — I cannot tell on what plane. There is nothing tangible to show for it and yet I am in good heart and my thoughts soar. Of course the pendulum will swing back and there will be other moods — the sort that made St Peter tremble at the wind and the waves.

*   *   *

I have a great yearning to talk to a few well-loved friends . . . when?

December 30th

Everything is still in the balance. Yesterday news filtered through by the grape vine that Bolz has been condemned. No one knows whether sentence has already been carried out or not. For endurance one has to rely on resources outside oneself. I find three great supports: *show forth thy mercy — we have trusted in thee — in patience you shall possess your souls.* Steadfastness really is a *virtue;* it is not merely temperament.

December 31st

The experience we are all passing through must surely at least produce one thing — a passionate love of God and desire for his glory. As far as I am concerned I find I have to approach him in a new and quite personal way. I must remove all the barriers that still stand between him and me, I must break down all the hidden reserve that keeps me from him. The prayer of van de Flue* must become a living reality. Divine life within me as faith,

---

* St. Nicholas of Flue, the patron saint of Switzerland.

hope and love. All this must combine with my temperament, abilities, faults, limitations, together with external circumstance to form a new mission, a pattern to whose realisation I am now pledged.

In a quiet hour tonight I will pass in review the year now ending, recollecting my personal acts in a prayer of repentance, of gratitude, of resignation, in short of trust and love.

I have to keep reminding myself what is happening and wonder whether I am suffering from hallucinations or self-deception. There can be no over-stating the seriousness of the situation and yet it all seems like a bad dream, quite unreal. Our Lord himself demanded that we should have the kind of faith that moves mountains, the trust that never fails. To him these were part of an infallible law which we can and must take seriously. Apart from the occasion when he drove the merchant from the temple we know of only one occasion on which he was really angry and that was when the apostles failed to heal the boy sick with the palsy because they had no confidence in their power. Surely we can remove by faith and prayer the one obstacle on which all this mistrust rests. When I think of the grace and the guidance vouchsafed to me in the past in spite of all that I have done . . .

*　　*　　*

It is difficult to sum up the year now ending in a few words. So much has happened during this year and yet I cannot see what its real message is for me, or its real achievement. Generally speaking it has not produced anything really effective. Hardship and hunger and violence have intensified and are all now more shattering than anyone could have imagined. The world lies in ruins round us. It is full of hatred and enmity. Everyone clings to their few miserable possessions because these are the last remaining things that they can really call their own.

Spiritually we seem to be in an enormous vacuum. Humanly speaking there is the same burning question – what is the point of it all? And in the end even that question sticks in one's throat. Scarcely anyone can see, or even guess at, the connection between the corpse-strewn battlefields, the heaps of rubble we live in and the collapse of the spiritual cosmos of our views and principles, the tattered residue of our moral and religious convictions as revealed by our behaviour. And even if the connection were fully understood it would be only a matter for academic interest, data to be noted and listed. No one would be shocked or deduce from the facts a need for reformation. We have already travelled so far in our progress towards anarchy and nihilism. Luckily powerful interests still oppose the hordes from across the Steppes for the world could not survive an alliance with them.

How can one assess the nations of today? Portugal is in a kind of sleeping beauty trance – foreigners will eventually decide her future. Spain will go into the melting pot again because she did not meet her last challenge squarely but solved the problem by cheating. Nowadays there is no room for feudalism even when it masquerades as people's tribunals. The only solutions are social ones. Spain has missed her chance to her eternal shame – and the shame of the Church too who stood by and made no protest. Italy has become purely objective. The transition from historical subject to historical object has hardly ever been made more quickly. Past guilt and ruptured loyalties make her suspect as a friend; no ally trusts her – quite apart from her people's inability to make history and the country's lack of historical genius from the modern point of view. Nothing was ever achieved in Italy without war and violence – and after all, all that's left is a few fine rather strained attitudes. Poland is paying a bitter penalty for her conceited pretensions and offences against other nations, particularly in the east. The Poles have never had much sense of reality though individually they are fine people. The Balkans lie at present in Russia's shadow. If as a result of all this suffering they should be at last welded into unity that would at least be one gain. For Hungary I fear a severer judgment. Many mistakes have been made there, particularly social ones. The Scandinavians are just waiting to see who will take them or force them to submit to foreign influence.

Russia is inscrutable. One really ought to visit Russia. Communism is nothing more than a donkey for an imperialism of limitless proportions. When Russia dreams she dreams magnificently and her fantasies are of unparalleled splendour. Possibly Communism needs the balance provided by Russia's interests. In any case a Russian-dominated Europe could not last long. Russia still has a great deal to learn – she is too indisciplined herself to rule others. The Slavs have not yet been absorbed by the west and are like a foreign body in the working of the machine. They can destroy and annihilate and carry away enormous quantities of booty but they cannot yet lead or build up. France is as disunited as ever, the moment western tension relaxes. Unless she joins hands with Germany she will go the way of Russia and fly to extremes. That England is on the down grade even I am beginning to believe. The English have lost their keenness and their spiritual gifts; the philosophy of materialism has eaten into England's bones and paralysed the muscles of her heart. The English still have great traditions and imposing forms and gestures; but what kind of men are they? The social problem has been overlooked in England – and also the problem of youth and the problem of America and of spiritual questions which can all too easily masquerade as cultural or political questions.

Germany on every plane is still struggling for its very existence. One thing is certain – there can be no Europe without Germany. And a Germany in which the original currents – Christianity, Germanism (*not* Teutonism) and classicism – no longer flow is not Germany at all and can be no help to the west. But here, quite apart from the outcome of the war, the more vital problem of bare subsistence plays a profoundly important part. In other words our problem too is a social one.

The picture of the west for the moment is decidedly grim. Foreign and arbitrary powers – Russia and America – are thrusting irresponsible hands into our lives from all directions.

Finally there are the Vatican and the Church to be considered. So far as concrete and visible influence goes the attitude of the Vatican is not what it was. It is not merely that it seems so because we get no information. Of course it will be shown eventually that the Pope did his duty and more, that he offered peace, that he explored all possibilities to bring about peace negotiations, that he proclaimed the spiritual conditions on which a just peace could be based, that he dispensed alms and was tireless in his work on behalf of prisoners of war, displaced persons, tracing missing relatives and so on – all this we know and posterity will have documentary evidence in plenty to show the full extent of the papal effort. But to a large extent all this good work may be taken for granted and also to a large extent it leads nowhere and has no real hope of achieving anything. That is the real root of the trouble – among all the protagonists in the tragic drama of the modern world there is not one who fundamentally cares in the least what the Church says or does. We overrated the Church's political machine and let it run on long after its essential driving power had ceased to function. It makes absolutely no difference so far the beneficial influence of the Church is concerned whether a state maintains diplomatic relations with the Vatican or not. The only thing that really matters is the inherent power of the Church as a religious force in the countries concerned.

This is where the mistake started; religion died, from various diseases, and man died with it. Or perhaps it is truer to say that man died of great possessions, of modern development, of the pace of modern life and so on – and religion died as man succumbed. In any case the west became a void so far as religion, as humanity and its spirit are concerned. In these circumstances how can any word or act on the part of the Church awaken the slightest echo in world affairs? The Church faces the same tasks that nations and states and the western world in general have to face – the problem of man, how he is to be housed and fed and how he can be employed in order to support himself. In other words we need social and economic regeneration. And then man also must be made aware of his true nature – in other words we need intellectual and religious regeneration. These are problems for the world, for individual states and nations, and they are also problems for the Church – far more so, for instance, than the question of liturgical forms. If these problems are solved without us, or to our disadvantage, then the whole of Europe will be lost to the Church, even if every altar faces the people and Gregorian chant is the rule in every parish. The supernatural demands a certain amount of expert action in regard to daily life, a degree of natural capacity for living without which life cannot survive. And the Church as an institution, an authority, requires a minimum of religious practice. Otherwise it can only have an idealistic value.

Therefore this year now ending leaves behind it a rich legacy of tasks and we must seriously consider how to tackle them. Above all else one thing is necessary – religious minded people must become more devout; their dedication must be extended and intensified.

And that brings me to my own affairs. Have I grown in stature in the past year? Have I increased my value to the community? How do things stand with me?

Outwardly they have never been worse. This is the first New Year I have ever approached without so much as a crust of bread to my name. I have absolutely nothing I can call my own. The only gesture of goodwill I have encountered is that the jailor has fastened my handcuffs so loosely that I can slip my left hand out entirely. The handcuffs hang from my right wrist so at least I am able to write. But I have to keep alert with one ear as it were glued to the door – heaven help me if they should catch me at work!

And undeniably I find myself in the very shadow of the scaffold. Unless I can disprove the accusations on every point I shall most certainly hang. The chances of this happening have never really seriously occupied my thoughts for long although naturally there have been moments of deep depression – handcuffs after all are a symbol of candidature for execution. I am in the power of the law which, in times like the present, is not a thing to be taken lightly.

An honest examination of conscience reveals much vanity, arrogance and self-esteem; and in the past also a certain amount of dishonesty. That was brought home to me when they called me a liar while I was being beaten up. They accused me of lying when they found I mentioned no names except those I knew they knew already. I prayed hard, asking God why he permitted me to be so brutally handled and then I saw that there was in my nature a tendency to pretend and deceive.

On this altar much has been consumed by fire and much has been melted and become pliable. It has been one of God's blessings, and one of the signs of his indwelling grace, that I have been so wonderfully helped in keeping my vows. He will, I am confident, extend his blessing to my outward existence as soon as I am ready for the next task with which he wishes to entrust me. From this outward activity and intensified inner light new passion will be born to give witness for the living God, for I have truly learned to know him in these days of trial and to feel his healing presence. *God alone suffices* is literally and absolutely true. And I must have a passionate belief in my mission to mankind, showing the way to a fuller life and encouraging the willing capacity for it. These things I will do wholeheartedly – *in nomine Domine*.

1945

January 1st
Jesus. The name of our Lord and of my Order shall be the first word I write in the New Year. The name stands for all the things I desire when I pray, believe and hope;

for inner and outer redemption; for relaxation of all the selfish tensions and limitations I place in the way of the free dialogue with God, all the barriers to voluntary partnership and surrender without reserve: and for a speedy release from these horrible fetters. The whole situation is so palpably unjust; things I have neither done nor even known about are keeping me here in prison.

The name Jesus stands also for all that I intended to do in the world, and still hope to do among mankind. To save, to stand by ready to give immediate help, to have goodwill towards all men, and to serve them. I still owe much to so many.

And in conclusion the Order, too, is embraced in my invocation of this name – the Order which has admitted me to its membership. May it be personified in me. I have pledged myself to Jesus as his loving comrade and blood-brother.

The Name stands for passionate faith, submission, selfless effort and service.

January 2nd
Next week, it seems, my fate will be finally decided. I am full of confidence; God lit an inner light in my soul at Christmas and it has revived my hope. I am already dreaming of my journey home, as excited as any school-boy. If nothing unexpected happens I shall be celebrating my last Mass before the trial on Friday, the feast of Epiphany.

My sister is very brave; I depend a lot on her prayers and her loyalty. I had not expected her to come until the end of the week.

Things still look very grim but I hope and pray. I have

learned a great deal in the past year. God seems much nearer and more real.

Recently I was reading Langbehn. He made it pretty difficult for people to see the truth he was proclaiming among all his general remarks. We used to rave about his work as students. My recent return to it was in many respects a farewell. The outstanding passages really ought to be extracted and collected in an anthology . . .

We are to be here two days more, then we go before the Gestapo. I shall keep the Sacrament with me until then so that I can go on celebrating Mass but I dare not take it with me then as I don't know how thoroughly we shall be searched there and the risk of desecration is too great.

To add to all the rest I have just learned that the presiding judge is anti-Catholic and a priest hater; yet another reason for leaving everything confidently in God's hands. It always comes back to this – only he can handle this situation.

During the daytime I read a little Eckhart, the only one of my books I have managed to retain. The whole Eckhart question would be simpler if people remembered that he was a mystic and his mind and soul and spirit were always soaring into higher spheres. He did his best to follow their flight in word and expression – but how can any ordinary mortal succeed in an undertaking that defied even St Paul? Eckhart failed as, in his own way, every man must fail when it is a matter of analysing and passing on an intimate personal experience: *individuum est ineffabile*. Once we have got back to the point where the ordinary man can have inexpressible secrets then a favoured few will emerge and God will find them sufficiently advanced to draw them into the creative dialogue as he drew Eckhart. With this in mind reading him becomes more rewarding and more comforting. It gives the reader a glimpse of the divine secret in every human heart.

Tomorrow morning I shall pass on this sheet and that there may not be any more before our fate is decided. To be quite honest if there were any way of escaping that day's ordeal I should seize it gladly, cowardly as that may sound. That's what it is to be weak! And everything depends on such trifles. The whole business really has no central theme — it just doesn't make sense. If N. sticks to his deposition — which is false — there is no hope at all. But what is the use of thinking about it — far better to kneel and pray placing everything in God's hands. *Ad majorem Dei gloriam.*

January 6th, the Epiphany

Thank God my fetters were so loosely fastened that tonight I could slip them off again. So I could celebrate Mass exactly as on Christmas Eve with my hands quite free. And this is the last night before the final stage and I am taking the Lord with me after all. The new hiding place the Marians have supplied me with is easily disposed of, so God will be with me during the proceedings.

Today the lawyer came to see me again. If all is to go well three things must happen. I have great confidence and my friends will not let me down. This is a moment in which the whole of existence is focused at one point and with it the sum total of reality. I must make my choice and take my stand. The reality of my faith, of God, of the world, of things and their interconnection, of responsibility and the willingness to be answerable for words and actions, as well as the inward urge to fight for existence: all these must be engaged in a single gigantic effort. I have prayed earnestly to God for both kinds of freedom and I shall do so again. After that I will read a little, or perhaps write a little more, till the night warder comes on his round. Then I have to pretend to be asleep.

Sometimes my own reactions puzzle me and I hardly recognise myself. How is it that I can live through these endless hours and days as if the whole wretched misery did not exist? It all seems so unreal. Very often I am not even conscious of it. Then suddenly it all comes back to me. Sometimes I feel like going raving mad and I have to pull myself together. I have to remind myself of the courage of my friends.

To be honest I am actually more afraid of the actual trial than its possible outcome. Although literally everything is in the balance I have complete confidence in life; and inwardly too I feel not the slightest temptation to despair.

January 7th
The only opportunity to pass anything on occurs just after exercise — hence just a few more lines.

Yesterday I was more absorbed in contemplating Leonardo da Vinci than the accusations brought against me. I really must study this many-sided and contradictory personality more closely. Many of the puzzling features of modern man seem to be encountered in him for the first time — but there are also a few clues for possible solutions.

*　　*　　*

The warder will soon be here. And tomorrow we are off to the 'house of silence'*. I wish my mother the joy of

---

* i.e., the Gestapo headquarters.

today's gospel and that speedily. She has borne enough of sorrow and sacrifice by now. *In the name of the Lord.* I have not written any farewell letters; my innermost feelings are beyond utterance.

MEDITATIONS

I THE PEOPLE OF ADVENT

Advent is the time for rousing. Man is shaken to the very depths, so that he may wake up to the truth of himself. The primary condition for a fruitful and rewarding Advent is renunciation, surrender. Man must let go of all his mistaken dreams, his conceited poses and arrogant gestures, all the pretences with which he hopes to deceive himself and others. If he fails to do this stark reality may take hold of him and rouse him forcibly in a way that will entail both anxiety and suffering.

The kind of awakening that literally shocks man's whole being is part and parcel of the Advent idea. A deep emotional experience like this is necessary to kindle the inner light which confirms the blessing and the promise of the Lord. A shattering awakening; that is the necessary preliminary. Life only begins when the whole framework is shaken. There can be no proper preparation without this. It is precisely in the shock of rousing while he is still deep in the helpless, semi-conscious state, in the pitiable weakness of that borderland between sleep and waking, that man finds the golden thread which binds earth to heaven and gives the benighted soul some inkling of the fulness it is capable of realising and is called upon to realise.

We ought not to ignore Advent meditations such as these. We have to listen, to keep watch, to let our heart quicken under the impulse of the indwelling Spirit. Only in this quiescent state can the true blessing of Advent be experienced and then we shall also recognise it in other ways. Once awakened to an inner awareness we are constantly surprised by symbols bearing the Advent message, figures of tried and proved personalities that bring out in a most forceful way the inner meaning of the feast and emphasise its blessing.

I am thinking of three in particular – the man crying in the wilderness, the herald angel, and our blessed Lady.

The man crying in the wilderness. We live in an age that has every right to consider itself no wilderness. But woe to any age in which the voice crying in the wilderness can no longer be heard because the noises of everyday life drown it — or restrictions forbid it – or it is lost in the hurry and turmoil of 'progress' – or simply stifled by authority, misled by fear and cowardice. Then the destructive weeds will spread so suddenly and rapidly that the word 'wilderness' will recur to men's minds willy-nilly. I believe we are no strangers to this discovery.

Yet for all this, where are the voices that should ring out in protest and accusation? There should never be any lack of prophets like John the Baptist in the kaleidoscope of life at any period; brave men inspired by the dynamic compulsion of the mission to which they are dedicated, true witnesses following the lead of their hearts and endowed with clear vision and unerring judgment. Such men do not cry out for the sake of making a noise or the pleasure of hearing their own voices, or because they envy other men the good things which have not come their way on account of their singular attitude towards life. They are above envy and have a solace known only to those who have crossed both the inner and outer borders of existence. Such men proclaim the message of healing and salvation. They warn man of his chance, because they can already feel the ground heaving beneath their feet, feel the beams cracking and the great mountains shuddering inwardly and the stars swinging in space. They cry out to man, urging him to save himself by a change of heart before the coming of the catastrophes threatening to overwhelm him.

Oh God, surely enough people nowadays know what it means to clear away bomb dust and rubble of destruction, making the rough places smooth again. They will know it for many years to come with this labour weighing on them. Oh may the arresting voices of the wilderness ring out warning mankind in good time that ruin and devastation actually spread from within. May the Advent figure of St John the Baptist, the incorruptible herald and teacher in God's name, be no longer a stranger in our own wilderness. Much depends on such symbolic figures in our lives. For how shall we hear if there are none to cry out, none whose voice can rise above the tumult of violence and destruction, the false clamour that deafens us to reality?

The herald angel. Never have I entered on Advent so vitally and intensely alert as I am now. When I pace my cell, up and down, three paces one way and three the other, my hands manacled, an unknown fate in front of me, then the tidings of our Lord's coming to redeem the world and deliver it have quite a different and much more vivid meaning. And my mind keeps going back to the angel someone gave me as a present during Advent two or three years ago. It bore the inscription: 'Be of good cheer. The Lord is near.' A bomb destroyed it. The same bomb killed the donor and I often have the feeling that he is rendering me some heavenly aid. It would be impossible to endure the horror of these times – like the horror of life itself, could we only see it clearly enough – if there were not this other knowledge which constantly buoys us up and gives us strength: the knowledge of the promises that have been given and fulfilled. And the awareness of the angels of good tidings, uttering their blessed messages in the midst of all this trouble and sowing the seed of blessing where it will sprout in the middle of the night. The angels of Advent are not the bright jubilant beings who trumpet the tidings of fulfilment to a waiting world. Quiet and unseen they enter our shabby rooms and our hearts as they did of old. In the silence of night they pose God's questions and proclaim the wonders of him with whom all things are possible.

Advent, even when things are going wrong, is a period from which a message can be drawn. May the time never come when men forget about the good tidings and promises, when, so immured within the four walls of their prison that their very eyes are dimmed, they see nothing but grey days through barred windows placed too high to see out of. May the time never come when mankind no longer hears the soft footsteps of the herald angel, or his cheering words that penetrate the soul. Should such a time come all will be lost. Then indeed we shall be living in bankruptcy and hope will die in our hearts. For the first thing man must do if he wants to raise himself out of this sterile life is to open his heart to the golden seed which God's angels are waiting to sow in it. And one other thing; he must himself throughout these grey days go forth as a bringer of glad tidings. There is so much despair that cries out for comfort; there is so much faint courage that needs to be reinforced; there is so much perplexity that yearns for reasons and meanings. God's messengers, who have themselves reaped the fruits of divine seeds sown even in the darkest hours, know how to wait for the fulness of harvest. Patience and faith are needed, not because we believe in the earth, or in our stars, or our temperament or our good disposition, but because we have received the message of God's herald angel and have ourselves encountered him.

Our blessed Lady. She is the most comforting of all the Advent figures. The fact that the angel's annunciation found a motherly heart ready to receive the Word, and that it grew beyond its earthly environment to the very heights of heaven, is the holiest of all Advent consolations. What use are all the lessons learned through our suffering and misery if no bridge can be thrown from our side to the other shore? What is the point of our revulsion from error and fear if it brings no enlightenment, does not penetrate the darkness and dispel it? What use is it shuddering at the world's coldness, which all the time grows more intense, if we cannot discover the grace to conjure up visions of better conditions?

Authors of legends and fairy tales have always used mothers as a favourite theme for rousing the strongest human feelings. Often these authors use motherhood as the symbol of the earth's fertility. They have even glamourised the hidden brood chambers of the eel in stream beds, identifying them with the mysterious up-surging of new life. Behind this symbolism lies a universal hunger and yearning, a premonition of the Advent-like expectation of our blessed Lady. That God should have condescended to become a human mother's son; that one woman whose womb was sanctified as the holy temple and tabernacle of the living God should have been permitted to walk the earth – these wonders make up the sum-total of the earth's actual purpose and they are the fulfilment of all its expectations.

Our eyes rest on the veiled form of the blessed, expectant Mary, and so many different kinds of consolation radiate from her. How great a gift this was to be bestowed on the earth that it might bring forth such fruit. What a miracle that the world should have been permitted to present itself before God in the shape of this laden warmth, the trustful security of a mother's heart.

On the grey horizon eventually light will dawn. The foreground is very obtrusive; it asserts itself so firmly with its noise and bustle but it does not really amount to much. The things that really matter are farther off – there conditions are different. The woman has conceived a child, has carried it in her womb and has brought forth a son and thereby the world has passed under a new law. You see this is not just a sequence of historical events that stand out in isolation. It is a symbol of the new order of things that affects the whole of our life and every phase of our being.

Today we must have the courage to look on our Lady as a symbolic figure. At their core these times through which we are living also carry the blessing and the mystery of God. It is only a matter of waiting and of knowing how to wait until the hour has struck.

Advent in three holy and symbolic forms. It is not meant as a flight of fancy but as a message addressed to me and to you, reader, if ever these pages find you. Its purpose is not good prose but an exposition of truth which we must refer to again and again as a standard and a source of encouragement when the burden of these dreadful days becomes too heavy and confusing.

Let us pray for receptive and willing hearts that the warnings God sends us may penetrate our minds and help us to overcome the wilderness of this life. Let us have the courage to take the words of the Messenger to heart and not ignore them, lest those who are our executioners today may at some future time be our accusers for the suppression of truth.

And let us kneel and pray for clear vision, that we may recognise God's messenger when he comes, and willing hearts to understand the words of warning. The world is greater than the burden it bears, and life is more than the sum-total of its grey days. The golden threads of reality are already shining through; if we look we can see them everywhere. Let us never forget this; we must be our own comforters. The man who promotes hope is himself a man of promise, of whom much may be expected.

And once again let us pray for faith in the maternal blessing of life as symbolised by our Lady of Nazareth. Life has to hold its own against ruthless and tyrannical forces, not only today but at all times. Let us have patience and wait in the spirit of Advent for that hour in which it shall please God to reveal himself anew. It may be in the very darkest hour – as the fruit and the mystery of these terrible times.

The air still vibrates with the noise of violence and destruction, of impudence and conceit, of weeping and despair. But silently the eternal values are gathering on the horizon. They are like the first pale rays of light as the promise of radiant fulfilment creeps upward accompanied by the first tentative notes of jubilation. It is not yet a full chorus but only an indication, a hint, far away. But it is drawing nearer. That is all for today; but for

27

tomorrow the angels will joyfully proclaim the event and we shall be happy if we have believed and faithfully trusted in the Advent.

II THE SUNDAYS OF ADVENT

First Sunday

Unless a man has been shocked to his depths at himself and the things he is capable of, as well as at the failings of humanity as a whole, he cannot possibly understand the full import of Advent.

If the whole message of the coming of God, of the day of salvation, of approaching redemption, is to seem more than a divinely-inspired legend or a bit of poetic fiction two things must be accepted unreservedly.

First, that life is both powerless and futile in so far as by itself it has neither purpose nor fulfilment. It is powerless and futile within its own range of existence and also as a consequence of sin. To this must be added the rider that life clearly demands both purpose and fulfilment.

Secondly it must be recognised that it is God's alliance with man, his being on our side, ranging himself with us, that corrects this state of meaningless futility. It is necessary to be conscious of God's decision to enlarge the boundaries of his own supreme existence by condescending to share our's for the overcoming of sin.

It follows that life, fundamentally, is a continuous Advent; hunger and thirst and awareness of lack involve movement towards fulfilment. But this also means that in his progress towards fulfilment man is vulnerable; he is perpetually moving towards, and is capable of receiving, the ultimate revelation with all the pain inseparable from that achievement.

While time lasts there can be no end to it all and to try to bring the quest to an ultimate conclusion is one of the illusory temptations to which human nature is exposed. In fact hunger and thirst and wandering in the wilderness and perpetual rescue by a sort of life-line are all part of the ordinary hazards of human existence.

God's promises are given to meet and deal with all these contingencies – not merely to satisfy man's arrogance and conceit. All we have to rely on is the fact that these promises have been given and that they will be kept. We are bound to depend on them – 'the truth shall set you free'. That is the ultimate theme of life. All else is mere explanation, compromise, application, continuation, proof, practice. God help us to find ourselves and then to get away from ourselves, back to him. Any attempt to live by other principles is bound to fail – it is a living lie. This is the mistake we have made as a race and as a nation and are now paying for so bitterly. We have committed an unpardonable sin against our own being and the only way to correct it is through an existential reverse - back again to truth.

But this reverse, this return, must be made *now*. *The threatening dangers of our sins.* Recognising the truth of existence and loosening the stranglehold of this error are not matters that can be postponed to suit our convenience. They call for immediate action because untruth is both dangerous and destructive. It has already rent our souls, destroyed our people, laid waste our land and our cities; it has already caused another generation to bleed to death.

None that wait on thee shall be confounded. We must recognise and acknowledge the hunger and thirst for satisfaction outside ourselves. After all it is not a case of waiting for something that may not happen. We have the comforting assurance of all those who wait knowing that the one they expect is already on the way.

If we are terrified by the dawning realisation of our true condition, that terror is completely calmed by the certain knowledge that God is on the way and actually approaching. Our fate, no matter how much it may be entwined with the inescapable logic of circumstance, is still nothing more than the way to God, the way the Lord has chosen for the ultimate consummation of his purpose, for his permanent ends. *Lift up your heads because your redemption is at hand.*

Just as falsehood entered the world through the heart and destroyed it, so truth begins its healing work there.

Light the candles quietly, such candles as you possess, wherever you are. They are the appropriate symbol for all that must happen in Advent if we are to live.

Second Sunday: Rise and stand on high

The value or worthlessness of human life, its profundity or shallowness, depends very much on the conditions of our existence. Life ought to preserve its real stature and not dissipate itself in superficial interests or empty sterility. Western civilisation is responsible for much misconception, foreshortening of views, distortion and so on both in public and personal life. We are the products of that faulty outlook. Distortion is a danger inherent in man's nature to which we as a generation seem to have been more than ordinarily prone.

Moments of grace, both historical and personal, are invariably linked with an awakening and restoration of genuine order and truth. That, too, is part of the meaning of Advent. Not merely a promise, but conversion, change. Plato would have said preparation for the reception of truth. St John more simply called it a change of heart. The prayers and the message of Advent shake a man out of his complacency and make him more vividly aware of all that is transmutable and dramatic in his life.

The first Sunday in Advent has the shock of awakening as its theme; it is concerned with underlining man's helplessness (the gospel), his turning towards God the pivot of his life (introit, epistle, gradual, offertory), his appeal for divine freedom which will recompense his helpless movement of surrender (the collect: *stir up thy might* . . .).

The second Sunday carries these thoughts a stage further making them more concrete through the exercise of personal will. The message of this second Sunday can be divided into three parts: first, affirmation, emphasising God's reaching out towards man. God is always the one who approaches. Not just occasionally but all the time (introit, epistle, gospel, secret). Affirming that he comes for our healing and salvation (introit, epistle, the first half); the injunction to man to take God seriously; the man who trusts in God will be steadfast and equal to whatever is demanded of him.

Second – all this is not a simplification or a neutralisation of life. God's blessing while giving man the pleasure of freedom does not relieve him of responsibility. The encounter with God is not of man's choosing either in regard to the place or the manner of it. Therefore the central portion of the message runs: 'Blessed is he that shall not be scandalised in me'. That is to say God is approaching but in his own way. The man who insists that his salvation shall depend on his own idea of what is right and proper is lost. It means further that the starting point of the movement towards salvation is the point at which contact is made with Christ. The way to salvation in the world is the way of the Saviour. There is no other way. We have to see this clearly and constantly affirm it.

Third, the keynote of this Sunday is the *decision*, the deliberate choice of salvation in Christ. Decision regarding the after-life (post communion); this love of heavenly things is a difficult and weighty matter. Decision in favour of freedom from minor entanglements and points of view—arise and stand on high (communion); the heights determine the range of vision and the air a soul may breathe. Decision as to character and behaviour (gospel, the figure of the man, John). Decision regarding one's duty as a Christian; our salvation depends upon our leading a Christian life which cannot be separated from personal obligation to the figure and the mission of Christ (gospel, collect). Decision to let the grace of God work in us (collect: *stir up our hearts*, the companion piece to *stir up thy might* on the previous Sunday), that God may dissolve our opposition and render us worthy to receive him and to execute his mission.

So this Sunday we must again fold our hands and kneel humbly before God in order that his salvation may be active in us and that we may be worthy to call upon him and be touched by his presence. The arrogance so typical of modern man is deflated here; at the same time the icy loneliness and helplessness in which we are frozen melts under the divine warmth that fills and blesses us.

Third Sunday: True happiness
What actually is happiness, true happiness? Philosophers have defined it as contentment with one's lot. That definition may fit certain aspects of the happy state but it certainly does not describe true happiness. If it did how

could I possibly be happy in my present circumstances?

As a matter of fact we may ask ourselves whether it is worth-while wasting time on an analysis of happiness. Is happiness not one of the luxuries of life for which no room can be found in the narrow strip of privacy which is all we have left when war occupies almost the whole of our attention? Certainly it would seem to be so in a prison cell, a space covered by three paces in each direction, one's hands fettered, one's heart filled with longings, one's head full of problems and worries.

Yet it does happen, even under these circumstances, that every now and then my whole being is flooded with pulsating life and my heart can scarcely contain the delirious joy there is in it. Suddenly, without any cause that I can perceive, without knowing why or by what right, my spirits soar again and there is not a doubt in my mind that all the promises hold good. This may sometimes be merely a reaction my defence mechanism sets up to counter depression. But not always. Sometimes it is due to a premonition of good tidings. It happened now and then in our community during a period of hardship and nearly always it was followed by an unexpected gift due to the resourcefulness of some kind soul at a time when such gifts were not customary.

But this happiness I am speaking of is something quite different. There are times when one is curiously uplifted by a sense of inner exaltation and comfort. Outwardly nothing is changed. The hopelessness of the situation remains only too obvious; yet one can face it undismayed. One is content to leave everything in God's hands. And that is the whole point. Happiness in this life is inextricably mixed with God. Fellow creatures can be the means of giving us much pleasure and of creating conditions which are comfortable and delightful, but the success of this depends upon the extent to which the recipient is capable of recognising the good and accepting it. And even this capacity is dependent on man's relationship with God.

Only in God is man capable of living fully. Without God he is permanently sick. His sickness affects both his happiness and his capacity for happiness. That is why, when he still had time for leisure man made so much noise about his happiness. And in the end even that was forbidden. Man's world became a prison which claimed him so completely that even happiness was made an excuse for further encroachment on his liberty.

In order to be capable of leading a full life man must stand in a certain relationship to God and obey certain rules. And the capacity for true happiness and joyful living is also dependent on certain conditions of human life, on a serious attitude towards God. Where life does not unfold in communion with God it becomes grey and sordid, calculating and joyless.

How must we live in order to be, or to become, capable of happiness? The question is one which ought to occupy us nowadays more than ever before. Man should take his happiness as seriously as he takes himself. And he ought to believe God and his own heart when, even in distress and trouble, he has an intuitive feeling that he was created for happiness. But this entails certain clear convictions. For a full and satisfying life man must know what it is all about. He must have no doubts about being on the right road with all the saints to back him up, and divine strength to support him. Such a life is a dedicated one, conscious of being blessed and touched by God himself.

How must a man live in order that happiness may overflow his heart and shine from his eyes, making his countenance radiant? How must he live to ensure that the work of his hands, conscientiously competent, will be crowned with success?

The liturgy for today, the third Sunday in Advent, gives us five conditions for the achievement of happiness and the capacity to enjoy it. In weighing up these conditions we have to examine our conscience and at the same time meditate on some of the historical causes for joylessness in modern life. We have to ask ourselves how it comes about that humanity has been fobbed off with a substitute so blatant that, were they not soul-sick, right thinking men would never have been taken in by it. Perhaps too this will give us an inkling of how matters stood with great men of the past who were really capable of happiness – whose eyes were so clear that they detected happiness everywhere. The sun song of St Francis is not a lyrical dream but a creative expression of that inner freedom which made it possible for him to extract the last ounce of pleasure from every experience and to perceive it in the successful issue of everything he undertook.

The conditions of happiness have nothing whatever to do with outward existence. They are exclusively dependent on man's inner attitude and steadfastness, which enable him, even in the most trying circumstances, to form at least a notion of what life is about.

* * *

For the first essential condition for true happiness today's liturgy turns to St Paul: *Rejoice. Rejoice in the Lord . . . the Lord is nigh.* Piety and happiness are closely interwoven. The question of piety and joyous fulfilment (or a joyless waste and void) both in personal life and in cultural tradition seem to the thoughtful mind so closely interwoven as to be inextricable.

They are linked in a double sense. To begin with, in the sense of the first commandment. Life comes under the control, and must conform to the order of, eternal laws. It is bound up with eternal values and meanings. *The Lord is nigh.* This is not merely one of the things a man should memorise, part of the repository of truth he needs to be constantly reminded of from the pulpit. It should be so completely absorbed as to become part of his consciousness. Thus absorbed it forms part of the tension which substantiates man's existence as an eternal being. Truth is not a haphazard collection of discoveries man makes in the course of manifold experiences; it is an order ratified by the Church. False values never cease importuning to wean man from this order, but by steadfastness in his belief he defeats the snares that beset him. Or at least he secures a firm foothold from which to defend himself.

A Godless life is one delivered up to a vast army of kill-joys. When man loses touch with the eternal truths he gets submerged in the weeds that sprout all over the garden of his life. They are senseless trivialities that assume an air of real importance. Though they pretend to have a purpose they are quite futile, and merely add obscurity and confusion to a life which is gradually engulfed in a sort of eternal twilight without light or direction. Torn between the claims of inconsistent and conflicting values man loses his taste for the exact standards set up by the Church and, deprived of guidance, sinks into a barbarism which proclaims the loudest attractions as being most worthy of approval, even though they are quite worthless. Hunted and driven and bewitched he is no longer master of his own fate, no longer a free man. It is hard enough to meet the ordinary hazards incidental to every existence; but the Godless man has no defences and is delivered up, bound and disarmed. Left to cope with them in this defenceless fashion he falls back on the excuse that fate is against him and the world is all wrong. He is a failure and it takes very little to keep him bogged down in depression and despair. The world becomes a cheerless place, not worth living in, although there seems to be no way out of it. Or, on the other hand, he may persuade himself that a flippant attitude is the right one to adopt, and he seeks a cheap way out of his troubles by various forms of escapism. The great illusion begins, the age of noise and mass mentality and organised animation — 'circuses' — for crowds. Till at last the earth begins to quake and underground rumblings, which have been more or less effectively drowned by the surface uproar, imperatively assert themselves. Thunder crashes proclaiming the day of judgment.

That is the way a race, a nation, an individual, wandering in the wilderness, can go to hell in a life without happiness. One terrifying factor about such a state of affairs is that it gets progressively worse. People grow to hate one another, all creation is disrupted and the harmony of the spheres is shattered by an orgy of violence and destruction.

There is only one remedy for such a state; each man must return to God, listen to his inner voice, consciously make contact with him. The great conversion will invariably win a blessing, one which will make man's wilderness blossom. It will open up new perspectives and unseal forgotten springs. Man should aspire to true good and not seek to fill his life with mere sensual gratification. Aspiration involves renunciation; but no sooner has man shed the trappings of selfish desire than freedom and mastery are within his possession. A surrender without reserve is essential; then 'these things' are given back to him. His eyes are opened and acquire a new perception. His earth regains its fruitfulness under the healing streams, which strengthen him for his appointed tasks and give him mastery as they carry the ship of his life on its way.

That is the meaning of *rejoice in the Lord*. Separated from God we are cut off from the eternal current of life and everything withers. This cannot be too firmly impressed upon mankind; it is the most important message of today. Above all we who proclaim that message must know it ourselves, and give our hearts to it, setting an example.

And that brings me to the second sense in which piety and happiness are interwoven. *In the Lord*. It is not only because of divine law and order that God will, and must, perpetually rekindle the light of illumination for us. *The Lord is nigh:* God is personally here in our midst. The theological truths concerning providence and divine guidance, concerning his actual presence in us through divine grace must be correctly understood and must become a living reality. Only thus can man live through the hazards and mischances of workday and holiday, through sunshine and shadow, probing every eventuality to that inner core in which God reveals their mystery and true significance. His interrogation, his guidance, his leading, his chastisement, his judgment, his comfort, his help. This is the hidden and holy burden of all the experiences we undergo. Not only where churches remain standing will there be temples of God; they will rise wherever human hearts beat high in adoration, wherever knees are bent in prayer, wherever the spirit is receptive to divine inspiration, wherever man, loving and worshipping, finds and fulfils his true self. And man will discover that he is living God's life within himself, in his very heart's core, proving the truth of the words of great and intuitive men like Eckhart, St Augustine and the rest. He will arrive at a state of perception in which he realises that the Supreme Being actually resides within him. He will find himself and regain faith in his own dignity, his mission and his purpose in life precisely to the extent that he grasps the idea of his own life flowing forth within him from the mystery of God. In this realisation any disasters that may threaten and all despairing moods are overcome, completely disarmed from within. Evil is unmasked and deprived of all its seeming power.

Only when a man arrives at that state of mastery and freedom can he breathe freely. The world and life itself then owe him nothing for he lives with every fibre of his being. Life gives him all it has to offer because nothing less can match the prodigal abundance of divine love which is poured out to meet man's receptive heart the moment he opens it unreservedly. He regains the clear vision which enables him to perceive eternal glory in all things. It moves him to awe, thanksgiving and praise. Everything is endowed with an inner radiance because his heart and the work of his hands are touched by creative truth. Such a man cannot help being happy and extending happiness to others. *Rejoice.*

*　　*　　*

Man cannot attain a state of happiness without conversion, a complete re-orientation of his entire existence. It cannot be achieved by his own effort, it can only result from the supreme freedom which God bestows as soon as man ceases to hedge himself round with self sufficiency, isolation and arrogance. The question is: how can man cross the borderline of human limitation to that divine intimacy which calls for complete surrender, and in return gives him all the resources of the infinite? To find the answer we must turn to St John the Baptist, the man of Advent: *he confessed and did not deny . . . It is not I.* Man must know the truth about himself without equivocation; he must be brought to the point of absolute honesty before himself and before others. Again and again he will be tempted to stand on the pedestal of his own self esteem and this temptation must be overcome at all costs. He may cavort for a time on his high horse of vanity and self deception but sooner or later the animal will throw him and make off leaving him stranded in the wilderness. He must abandon the fictions he has laboured to polish so as to increase their plausibility.

An honest self appraisal combined with a sober summing up of one's own capacities and potentialities is the first step towards truth in life. *The truth shall set you free* — and freedom, in every part of life, is all that matters.

Man has a great tendency to lapse into dreams; he rarely stops dreaming. There are genuine creative dreams that entice him on and drive him out of the rut of routine. Woe to youth if it should ever lose its capacity to conjure up glorious visions and to feel the breath of the Holy Spirit. But there are also misleading and foolish dreams that bemuse the dreamer, weakening his judgment so that he cannot distinguish the false from the true. They prevent a man progressing by his own effort; they tempt him to have too good an opinion of his own powers — and on the level of absolute being such errors are fatal.

There are two tests by which a man can tell whether

41

the impulse moving him is genuine or not – the test of service and the test of proclamation of truth. St John is the guide again.

First, the warning voice. It reminds man of what he owes to his own integrity and helps him avoid becoming puffed up with pride and self sufficiency. It reminds him constantly that he is on this earth for a purpose. To discover that purpose and to fulfil it is his mission in life. The idea of service and a true sense of duty cannot be separated from a fruitful human existence; they are its very essence. Anyone who fails in these essentials makes a fundamental mistake and will never find the road to self knowledge. Duty and service may take many different concrete forms – but the emphasis must always remain constant.

The second test – *he it is*. Affirmation, testimony, praise of the Lord. In this supreme state of reverence man sheds his limitations; in this frame of mind he can arrive at complete honesty and absolute clarity of vision. It is not a thing that comes easily – it needs much practice. But it is the only state in which man is receptive to divine grace and it cannot be attained without considerable personal effort. He can only comprehend the great realities he is meant to comprehend by making a supreme effort.

* * *

Absolute honesty in regard to himself is essential because it keeps a man from sinking into a dream-like Nirvana in which he views his life with detachment and disinterest. Instead of dreaming he must be wide awake to prepare the way for progress in an active and upward direction. For this a receptive and selfless state of mind is necessary – a state in which precisely because it is selfless he finds a greater personal freedom than he had ever imagined possible. The attitude can best be summed up as one of obedient receptivity, selfless service, exultant gratitude. Personal limitations are shed like worn out garments and with them the anxiety that accompanies them. The world and its affairs are viewed with a new and far more penetrating insight. A long road must be travelled before man arrives at uninhibited contact with God, but it is the road – and the only road – to his own fulfilment. What he must recognise is that the whole process is entirely a personal one, can only be worked out in his individual existence, cannot be measured by outward events at all even though the trials he meets every day play their part in opening his eyes to the connection and significance of the happenings of his life. To aspire to a higher state is an inborn attribute of human nature. The man who is completely satisfied with things as they are and has no desire to rise above his limitations can only be described as spiritually mediocre, self centred, obtuse, pompous and narrow minded.

So for all the humility of self surrender man must still try to rise above himself – he must still have ambition. But a very different kind of ambition – not the usual arrogant, self-seeking kind. This is a genuine effort to meet human nature's inherent need to fulfil itself. Such dynamic principles underly human nature that its driving power must find an outlet. When the individual falls into the most dangerous of human errors, attempting to pose as a superman and so on, he reveals the mainspring of his nature just as clearly as if he were genuinely seeking to fulfil himself. In order to become more of a man he finds he has to be a man and so he is back at his starting point. Unless a man reaches out, letting his imagination soar, striving towards a high ideal, the only alternative is to vegetate – and a man who vegetates ends by becoming less than human. This is the psychological explanation of the great human tragedy through which we are passing today.

Here again – we must be honest with ourselves. The great freedom cannot be won without drastic action, certainly, but our approach must be co-operative, never defiant, challenging or demanding. The fire of Prometheus is a fable: the divine fire is strong enough and efficient enough in its action to command our respect without any theatrical gestures of violence and vengeance to deck out its power and effectiveness. The Lord is not a vengeful God; he is himself and anyone who fails to recognise this is preparing for himself a burden under whose weight he is eventually bound to collapse. Man's contribution to the attainment of the great freedom consists of an honest personal assessment, an open and receptive heart, willing obedience combined with readiness to serve and genuine acknowledgment of God – that is to say thanksgiving and praise. The man who approaches Advent in this frame of mind will experience the supreme encounter and the resultant liberation, for God gives freedom to those who make his coming their own personal experience, with all the comfort and support that experience conveys.

Thou hast blessed thy land . . . and turned away the captivity: stir up thy might and come . . . (introit, collect, offertory, post communion). All these are pointers to God's intervention in the affairs of mankind and thus to the benefits that result. But the fundamental attitude on man's part is essential – he must fulfil this condition before the benefits can be received.

The attitude is one of complete surrender even to the point of ignoring all outward distractions. The liturgy calls this state *captivitas* – captivity – and *iniquitas* – guilt. Man is only capable of ultimately realising his true self by the direct intervention of God, who breaks the fetters, absolves the guilt and bestows the inevitable blessing. For the moment I am not in the least concerned with how a man arrives at this state. But what I am concerned with, what concerns us all, most urgently, is the resigned, shoulder shrugging indifference of modern man to these vital issues – and the fact that this attitude seems to be accepted by the Church. Because this indifference only increases the material problems and makes them appear ever more insoluble, it ought to make us stop and think and try to produce some constructive results. One has the impression almost of being lost in a vast forest with every step leading farther and farther into the depths however hard one looks for the way out. Sooner or later we all make the discovery that human beings are subject to prohibitions and restraints that are even harsher, more irksome and more inexorable than the limitations of nature. The liturgy calls this imprisonment – a word we often use very glibly, for only those who have actually suffered it can have any idea of the effect it has on one's inner nature. The man who has had a taste of prison life knows what it means to be shut up in a narrow cell, his wrists fettered, his mind occupied with a thousand depressing thoughts as he visualises the flag of freedom drooping forgotten in some obscure corner. Again and again his hopes rise only to fall back into despair when the steps of the warder approach or the key grates harshly in the lock. Then dreams fade into reality and it all seems hopeless. Again and again you come back to the same point – you have no key, and even if you had there is no keyhole on the inside of a prison door. And the window is barred and it is so high up you can't even look out. Unless someone from the outside comes to set you free there can be no end to your misery – all the will power in the world makes no difference. The facts clamour for recognition.

And when you think about it this is precisely the state mankind as a whole is in today. Man has become incapable of living fully because he has not found divine freedom. I know perfectly well that only God can unlock the handcuffs and open that door and that his creative power could make me free again in the eyes of the world. Man's condition in general is just like mine. What he needs is a new awareness of the gospel, the good tidings so that he may *really* hear and understand. He needs an open, receptive mind – God will not force any man to accept salvation. We must keep on reminding modern man that God stands at the door, ready and waiting, but that man himself must open the door. The grim happenings round us – the devastation and violence – are not exaggerated rumour but solid fact. And God's knock at the door of our spirit, his invitation to surrender to him and accept in return his freedom, is a thing that should be taken just as seriously.

On one point let there be no misunderstanding – left to ourselves with only our own strength to rely on, we shall never find freedom. The text about man's not being able to call a foot of earth his own is an exact picture of our helplessness on a purely human level. Where divine freedom is concerned there is no question of bargaining, of exchanging one set of chains for another as is the case in human affairs. With God the only way to complete freedom is complete surrender — there is no alternative. But his summons are always creative.

The indispensable preparation on man's part is a change of heart. We must re-order our lives. And it is desperately urgent that we do it *now* and do not try to put it off. We must make a complete surrender of ourselves, not in a sudden rush of emotion which is likely to be as transitory as it is violent, but wholly and continually until placing ourselves in God's hands has become habitual and permanent. Only then can God's will for our own liberation and salvation be done in us. And for western man particularly this change of heart is something very urgently needed — it has become a question of life and death not only for his eternal well-being but for his very existence here on earth. The whole future of history — whose sole purpose really is the glory of God — depends on western man's regaining his freedom, on his battling his way through the wilderness to the open sea.

And it is all so intimately linked with man's desire and capacity for happiness. Only the man capable of seeing ultimate truth and being saved by it can experience real joy. Freedom is truly the breath of life. We sit in damp dug-outs and shelters and cells, gasping in the foul air and reeling under fate's devastating blows. It is time we stopped attributing false values to things, glamourising them. We should see things as they really are. Our present life is bankrupt. And if we really admit this then already there is a faint foreshadowing of change — a slight lessening of tension, a gradual calming of the beating of our hearts. The clank of chains loses its grating harshness in response to prayer. *Drop dew ye heavens* . . . we really need to go into things deeply, to see the connecting link between them, to call on God our Saviour for deliverance

47

from the evil that is oppressing us. Then we shall discover freedom, though at first it may only be elbow room; the walls of our cell will open out and we shall breathe more easily; the horizon will beckon with promise. The weeping and wailing may still go on but a new undertone of yearning, of understanding, of joy, seems to filter through the broken voices of the sorrowing multitude.

Once a man has attained inner knowledge and freedom ordinary annoyances and unexpected happenings lose their power to disturb. He can stand back and look at things dispassionately, with detachment, not in cold, calculating appraisal but with the kindly glance of the man who is in control of the situation. And such a man is not easily disturbed, whatever happens. *Be in nothing solicitous* — the epistle applies this to the freedom man achieves when he forsakes the hectic rush of burdened days, tight schedules and feverish haste. Decisions can be made without hesitation because he has clearer insight. Situations can be assessed correctly because all the implications are at once clear. In this state of freedom the healing, creative power of God and the restless, adventurous impulse of man meet and bear fruit. The need is still there but the anguish has gone; the burden still has to be carried but the shoulders are stronger; the struggle for existence continues but without the constant anxiety. St Paul reminds us that man has certain characteristics and that certain conditions are most natural to him — to love, for instance, is one; to adore is another. And St Paul lists others including gratitude, reverence, prayerful hope. The man who, in his inner being, has entered into the perfect relationship with God fulfils the real purpose of his existence; from that point on the dialogue can begin. Such a man discovers his real self because he has first put his mind in order. Long-forgotten talents, and some that have atrophied for want of use, are brought to life again. His whole being grows – his eyes are clearer and keener and he feels more sure of himself in spite of constant lapses and moods of depression. He is still at the testing stage but he is beginning to get over the worst. His soul begins to sing and he has a vague awareness of the stirring of deep fountains . . . until eventually he comes to the full realisation of the truth *in the Lord*. And the day will come when the singing soul will be ready to join in the ultimate alleluia.

All this is true – provided man takes the essential first step of relinquishing his personal self of his own free will. Only thus can he come to the necessary state of receptivity. It is an attitude conditioned by the relationship of the creature to the Creator, and the only attitude in which man can bear the reality and the overwhelming bliss of God's presence. For the fully-awakened consciousness that knows and believes, this bliss is sufficient reward in itself. But it is really only a foretaste; it allows a man to get his breath back ready for the next step, and the constantly increasing wonder of the experience keeps the soul alert.

Thus life goes on to reach to its furthest horizons and supreme hour. Never do the promises cease to beckon. Isaias's wonderful words, in the communion prayer, are addressed to everyone: 'Say to the faint hearted – take courage and fear not'. They heal the deepest wounds and bring comfort and solace to the most cheerless situations. Woe to the world and to all humanity if it ever ceases to believe in the promises. Without them there can be no life; all splendour, all courage and all joy will be at an end. If belief in them dies, happiness dies also.

God's promises are always before us; they are more constant than the stars, more effective than the sun; they heal us and set us free. They transform us and widen the compass of our existence to infinity. In the face of the promises even grief loses its bitterness; trouble discloses inner courage and in loneliness is sown the seed of trust.

And what about the 'good cheer' we are told of and which we so much want to share? I have said nothing about the exciting kinds of happiness that can flood one's whole being with nothing to stimulate it except the simple everyday gifts God in his goodness bestows upon us. Warm sun; the glint of light on moving water; the prodigal exuberance of spring flowers; meeting another human being who is sincere and with whom we have an immediate understanding. Nor have I dwelt on the emotional impulse that expresses itself in true love or true sorrow, the way in which both heaven and earth can give us cause for great and profound happiness. I have not mentioned these – I know very well that happiness can come from so many sources and that all of them can suddenly dry up. But I am not concerned with these things. I am only concerned with what has become now a familiar theme in my own life, the nearness of God and the divine order which alone can heal man's mortal ills. It is this – and only this – that can both fit him for happiness and give him the means to be happy. To restore divine order and proclaim God's presence – these have been my vocation, the task to which my life is dedicated.

Fourth Sunday: Binding and loosing
What is true of the Advent prayers applies also to Advent in life. Before the curtain rises and the scene is disclosed, stretching into infinity, expectation mounts in a crescendo

of excitement. Our confidence is well founded and so is the suspense of waiting because the promise is already fulfilled and its truth demonstrated. Day triumphs and the darkness shrinks back into nothingness – like the shadows in the wings when the stage is set as a temple of light. On the fourth Sunday in Advent the acute awareness of shrouded mystery is deepening for the final hour of darkness that heralds the dawn. There is an intense awareness of captivity, of crippling disability and despair, but it is already shot through with a premonition of divine grace – the premonition that will so soon become certainty.

The three laws of bondage
The law of guilt: 'Grace which is hindered by our sins' (collect).

All the jargon about 'fate', 'bad luck', having a life of misfortune and so on is dealt with in this one sentence. As we move from night to day we are beset with decisions the heart has to make and we ought to think about them very seriously for the whole outcome will depend on the choices we make. And this is true not only of individual personal lives but also of generations, races, epochs. Good and evil come from the same source; a false decision, a wrong inclination of our will and all that follows is doomed; the vision is clouded, the hands grow clumsy and the work they produce is malformed if not harmful. Or the complete opposite – a change of heart, illumination, repentance and a blessing that results in fruitful and productive work.

This is true of all our personal life. The events which affect us are doubly interwoven. In one way they are accidents that result from a logical sequence of causes which apparently we cannot escape. But their deeper significance as opportunities for the healing and cleansing of our soul is even more important. The whole art of assessing the value or worthlessness of our experiences and of events lies in knowing their existential significance and being willing to admit it. It gives man power to deal with anything fate may have in store. It allows him to penetrate to the inner meaning of things and the moment the meaning of anything is clear it ceases to be mysterious – it 'makes sense'. And with this weapon man can strike the hardest, coldest, most unyielding rocks and draw living water from them.

Today more than ever it is vital that this should be universally known and recognised. Life in our age has become so degenerate and unhealthy that even the natural obstacles are multiplied by widespread evil hampering and delaying the good. And there can be no escape from it except through a great conversion, a change of heart which like most true conversions will take place in silence growing until it is strong enough to break through the ice that clings to modern life and crushes it like a curse.

The law of history. No life is ever outside the scope of history or unsignificant for it. But there is no such thing as holy, or unholy, history. History is creative being in action. Development, unfolding, are processes of 'becoming' whether they are the result of an internal motive force or an external intervention, and they make up the sum-total of existence. Any attempt to escape history, to live outside it as it were, to run away from reality, only leads to illusion. Escapism and reaction have no place in real life.

The gospel for the fourth Sunday in Advent evokes history. It refers to the mighty who determine the structure of the small room in which the Light of the World will come into being, bringing salvation. In order to recognise that a moment of historical crisis is implied here, we have to clothe these names with the memory of the part they played in history. From the imperial throne to the holy of holies the outlook was hopeless; even the priesthood had been corrupted by power politics, family egoism and narrow-minded bigotry.

Hopeless — that is the iron with which history often seeks to fetter healing hands, breaking the hearts of the enlightened few and reducing them to trembling hesitancy or cheap silence or tired resignation. As Christians we ought to recognise these shackles of history for what they are; indeed to ignore them is sinful evasion. History does not have the last word but it is only through history that the decisive word can be carried into effect. If we fail to recognise this we are performing a masque before a graven image which deceives us, or with which we are trying to deceive ourselves, into a false sense of security.

The law of mysteries. Goethe says: if you want the eternal make the most of the temporal. The grand old man of Weimar spoke from a good deal of experience but he had no real personal metaphysical background. Borrowing freely from Spinosa's pantheistic logic he translated it into lyric form and made it sound like his own discovery. It would be hard to find a more sympathetic guide, or a more dogmatic one, than Goethe as far as essential conduct and values are concerned — despite the pleasure he took in accumulating experience and the liberty he boasted of. Schiller is different in that the tension springs mainly from his inability to reconcile Kant's ideas with Spinosa's.

But this is not really relevant. Reaching out to 'infinity

53

in all directions' contributes nothing ultimately to human knowledge except in conjunction with an already established *a priori*, or the recognition that there are limits to human perception and beyond them all is veiled and silent in unutterable mystery. It is precisely the road leading to the *finite* in all directions – which most great men have a talent for exploring – that makes one aware of the mystery surrounding us on every hand. Ultimately we have to concede that there are many questions to which we can find no answer and that there are countless things in heaven and earth for which we possess no explanation whatsoever.

Man would give a great deal to get rid of this thorn in his flesh, this great question mark which seems a reproach to his idea of a properly ordered existence. He may try to ignore it, to blunt his senses to the mysteries surrounding him and bury himself in the round of everyday reality; then one day an avalanche overwhelms him and he is driven from his secure little home and well-kept garden on to the highway of displaced persons, seeking a destination somewhere, somehow, and finding life very hard indeed. Or he may try to think up new categories from which he might possibly be able to wring an answer – categories of logic or emotion, of sense or nonsense. But whether he tackles the problem sceptically or with heroic optimism, whether he attacks it little by little or by main force, it always comes to the same thing in the end. He always has to plunge into more and more thought – the only respite from facing the seriousness of the situation and the hopelessness of ever finding adequate solutions to all the problems that remain unsolved.

The threads of which life is made up are too intricately interwoven for man to be able to separate them. Its burdens and its rewards are such that man, left to his own resources, can neither bear nor understand. When, after untold labour, he thinks he has reached the ultimate it always proves to be the penultimate; and so it goes on, always new signs, new missions, new information, new questions, new tasks. Hence despite the most vigilant care and all human endeavour, despite alertness and willingness, life remains an inscrutible mystery and often a disquieting one at that.

The three laws of freedom

A man only finds his true self when he rises above himself. Beyond his own natural resources he finds the strength and power to realise his potentialities and the freedom he needs to draw the breath of life – in other words he comes to self-realisation. Yet the ability to tap this source of strength and power depends on decisions which rest entirely with his own personal will and can only be made by him.

Overcoming the law of guilt. The power that will overcome the law of sin is not to be found within the heart of the sinner who seeks it. And he must first fulfil the necessary condition of a change of heart before he can even receive that redemptive power which lies beyond his reach. He must first call upon it and then make himself ready so that he may go to meet it. Advent does not offer freedom to the man who is convinced he is already converted. *Stir up thy power: by the help of thy grace.* It is a case of God against sin. Sin is very like a handcuff – only the person with the key can unlock it. It doesn't matter how fervently I desire it, I cannot rid myself of my handcuffs because I have no key. And sin is like the door of my cell – even if I had a key I could not unlock the door because it has no keyhole on this side. It can only be opened from outside. And opposed to sin is God, as accuser and judge if man is obstinate in error, as liberator and saviour if he will turn to his Redeemer and ally himself with his Creator against sin. But the recognition of this entails something else. We have come to a time when devout souls are much needed, souls who will pray for us all, lifting up our plight to God and ensuring by the inclination of their own hearts that others will be moved to do the same. The plea must swell to a clamour and must go on ceaselessly. We have to take God at his word – the laws of prayer are his own – cf. Matt. 21, 18; Luke 17, 5 and many other texts. The outcome of so many things, the occurrence of so many miracles depends on the wholeheartedness of our plea to God. He will not always provide sensational miracles – though they will occur now and again, witnessing to his divine power. But with truly regal bounty he will reveal himself in a thousand little everyday adjustments proving by innumerable apparently casual events that his will prevails in the end. The man of real faith has no doubt about the outcome – he leaves the means to God. And when God repays, and more than repays, man's trust we can only stand speechless in amazement and awe.

Now particularly is the time for prayers that will storm heaven. This is no Quietist dispensation from responsibility and action. On the contrary – there is a very stringent law regarding deeds and the time has come for that deed which is inherently blessed. We should remember St Ignatius's rule – it is the intention that matters. That is the rule for today. Intervention, action and achievement must come from devout prayer – that is perhaps truer today than it has ever been.

There is no cause for depression, resignation or despair in all this – rather it should give us greater confidence and spur us on to unrelenting effort. We must make a covenant with God against the evils that surround us: *show mercy on us for we have hoped in thee*. It is essential and is the measure of the demand that God makes of us. He is as near to us as our desire for him is sincere; his mercy is as great as the wholeheartedness of our appeal for it; his freedom is as real and imminent as our belief in him and in his coming is unshaken and unshakable. That is the truth.

Freedom from the law of history. The Holy Spirit, Almighty God, the Lord of all history is alone outside history, above it. But we must not delude ourselves that we can find freedom by running away from history. We have to find this freedom within the framework of history in alliance with God for the fulfilment of his purpose.

This is obvious if we look at the gospel. In the time when the historic situation was hopeless, even within the holy of holies, God's word went forth to John. We can picture what happened: the voice rang out and people were greatly disturbed. They flocked to Jordan where baptism promised the way to freedom. They heard the warning and prophecy of the great upheaval that was to prepare the way for the Messiah and a new life. Shutters were pulled down and windows thrown open – the whole horizon widened and John's mission was a success.

And history was fulfilled both by the withdrawal to the wilderness and the return to the highways to proclaim the message. The wilderness – John's wilderness – is not a place of escape, adding to the armour of our self-esteem; it is a place of preparation, a place for gathering our strength and collecting our thoughts, for re-arming ourselves, for listening expectantly for the word of command. Bodily preparation, immediate response to God's message, confidence and courage in passing it on – these are the things that safeguard history. They will culminate at the right historic hour – not just any hour one might wish or dream of – and when history unfolds in this way it is drawn back into the original order of creation which exists for the glory of God.

The word of God cannot be embraced in fetters, cannot be heard when all human values are chained in fear and frustration and fatigue and weighed down with the escapist urge to compromise. Prepare the way is the task that lies at the heart of history. Again and again history will surrender to the Word because history too knows its Master and cannot exist away from its true source.

Freedom from the law of mystery. This shackle too is loosened by the message of the fourth Sunday of Advent, and in three ways. First we are obliged to acknowledge the truth, that our life is full of mysteries. The ability to realise that there are mysteries and to endure them is a test to which man must submit. It is part of the act of adoration to acknowledge God, above and beyond, and to take him seriously even in the stress and strain of everyday life.

Then the message conveys the Christmas blessing reminding us that things are sanctified; that thanks to the presence of God and his immanence in creation particular mysteries do exist and that certain times and certain things transmit his blessing. The whole character of the feast has a grace-bestowing quality which is peculiarly typical.

Hold on and speak out: again a command, a mission. The night we are enduring is bound to yield to light; the chosen moment of history is bound to hear the tidings of the Redeemer.

Until he come: everything is concentrated in expectation, waiting and watching for the coming of the Lord. *He is the Lord* – the awareness of God in the midst of our life. The infinite value of steadfastness is stressed here – unremitting watchfulness touched by God and, because of that divine touch, capable of renewing itself time and time again, of remaining wakeful. *Until he come:* to keep on, to be forever on the way. That is the law that governs a truly free life.

God is day and night, bondage and freedom, prison cell and the whole world. The great encounter is only explicable thus. But man has to go on seeking for that explanation, putting question after question until they are all answered. God is the source of both question and answer and each answer must be followed up. The eve of Christmas is both a proclamation and a mission; a holy night and a night pregnant with promise. The wise, the watchers and those who bring tidings, men who know God and his order, those who watch expectantly and pray ceaselessly are those who will transform our fetters into a sacrament of freedom.

III THE VIGIL OF CHRISTMAS

Concerning the blessed burden of God
There has always been a lot of misunderstanding about
the feast of the nativity. Superficial familiarity, sentimental crib-making and so on have to some extent distorted
our view of the stupendous event the feast commemorates.

This year (1944) the temptation to make an idyllic
myth of Christmas will no doubt be less in evidence than
usual. The harsh realities of life have been brought home
to us as never before. Many who spend Christmas in
dug-outs and shelters that would make the stable at
Bethlehem seem cosy by comparison will have little
inclination to glamourise the ox and the ass. They may
even stumble on the idea of asking themselves what really
happened that holy night – was the world made a better,
a more beautiful place? Did life acquire a blessing because
the angels sang *Gloria in excelsis*, because the shepherds
were astounded and hurried to pay homage, because a
king lost his nerve and ordered the innocents to be
massacred? Yet at this point the questions have already
started to run wild – for this crime took place simply and
solely because it was the holy night.

Yet Christians probably never pray more fervently than
when they offer up the *respirare* at the conclusion of the
vigil Mass. We breathe again because the birth of the
Only-Begotten will, we trust, ease our burdens. A load
has been lifted from our hearts. Life takes on a new
meaning because a new perspective is disclosed, because
the decisive moment has been reached again, because the

relative security we normally count on has not yet been swallowed up by the uncertainties of this abnormal time.

To breathe again. To be honest I too long to be able to breathe again, to be relieved of my troubles. How earnestly I prayed the prayer for speedy deliverance in yesterday's Mass. Each day I have to steel myself for the hours of daylight and each night for the hours of darkness. In between I often kneel or sit before my silent Host and talk over with him the circumstances in which I am. Without this constant contact with him I should have despaired long ago.

The question that applies to the whole world applies to me personally and concretely on this feast of the nativity. Is there anything different about celebrating Mass here in this narrow cell where prayers are said and tears are shed and God is known, believed in and called on? At stated hours the key grates in the lock and my wrists are put back into handcuffs; at stated hours they are taken off – that goes on day after day, monotonously, without variation. Where does the breathing again which God makes possible come in? And the waiting and waiting for relief – how long? And to what end?

It is necessary to celebrate the feast of the nativity with great realism, otherwise one's imagination will conjure up magical happenings for which one's sober reason can discover no justification nor prospect. And as a result of that the celebration of the feast could easily lead to bitter disappointment and deep depression. The vigil Mass leads to the necessary restrained, expectant and realistic frame of mind in three ways.

God whose coming we celebrate is and remains the God of promises. At the introit we pray: *This day you shall know – and in the morning you shall see,* clearly referring to the

61

coming feast day and the connection between it and the vigil. But it also refers to a perpetual state, to the fundamental condition of our life. It is one of the most tragic and disturbing factors of our existence that we may know a great deal and have vast experience behind us and yet fail to find a place of shelter, a secure refuge. Man would so much like to regard his acquired knowledge as final, to make himself at home here and feel secure. But every now and then he grows uncomfortably aware of the fact that his wanderings are not yet over. Again and again the truth we believe we have grasped proves to be merely a prelude, an overture to something that lies beyond, beckoning and leading us onward. And man must go on, must continue his journey if he is to obtain life's reward. To call a halt before the end is reached means death, metaphysical and religious ruin.

This 'in the morning you shall see' absorbs the wholesome, creative unrest to which we owe all that is genuinely alive in our own make-up. But at what a price. The Lord calls it hunger and thirst after righteousness and one needs to have experienced the agony of counting the hours until the next ration of bread is due really to understand what this means and how much is expected of man in this eternal quest.

And the alternative? Indifference, resignation, insensitivity, loss of appetite, the atrophying of the organs, the loss of our spiritual nerve, over-strain and deadly fatigue -- in short one of those fatal wounds through which the life-blood of so many human beings nowadays is ebbing away. A man may think he can escape the curve of tension into which the law has forced him but in the end he comes to the realisation that burdens are part and parcel of the condition of life.

So now, on the threshold of Christmas which we like to approach as if it were a kind of earthly paradise, we come on the same motif: *you shall know* – you have received tidings: *you shall see* – you must be on your way to find real fulfilment in real encounter. Here again we have real tension, the theme of the bow which can only be stretched when the arrow is applied to it.

We ought to remember we are approaching the feast of God-made-man, not of man rendered divine. The divine mystery takes place on earth and follows the natural course of earthly events. As the epistle so emphatically states: *according to the flesh – from the seed of David*. It cannot be interpreted any other way. It is an indisputable but incomprehensible fact that God enters our homes, our existence, not only like us but actually as one of us. That is the unfathomable mystery. From this point on the Son is absorbed by history, his fate becomes part of history and history's fate is his fate. In the darkest cells and the loneliest prisons we can meet him; he is continually on the high roads and in the lanes. And this is the first blessing of the burden – that he is there to help us bear it. And the second blessing of it is that all we who have to bear it know at once when the strong shoulder is pushed under to relieve the weight. And the third blessing is that since that holy night when divine life and the original pattern of existence was born on earth, strength enabling us to master life has grown from that upsurge of divine vitality in human existence and is reflected in the existence of the community, to which he revealed himself.

We shall be better able to cope with life's demands if we remain constantly aware of the directions this night provides. Let us continue our journey along the highway of life without allowing ourselves to be deterred or frightened by occasional desolate stretches. A new spirit has entered into us and we will not waver in our belief in the star of the promises or weary of acknowledging the angels' *Gloria* even if we sometimes have tears in our eyes as we join in. Many disasters have been turned into blessings because men have risen above them.

God in the Christmas encounter is still the challenging God. The greatest misconceptions all centre round the typical Christmas picture of God. Here too man is so wrapped up in appearances that the breath-taking terrible reality of the birth of God as a human child scarcely enters his mind and the soul doesn't grasp its significance. The truth is too tremendous to be appreciated unless one concentrates on it fully. Of course the externals – the sweetly sentimental pictures, the carols, the cribs and so on are a comfort both to mankind as a whole and to the individual. But there is a great deal more to the nativity than that. The comfort man derives from the externals is only the symbol of the far greater gifts this event, and the feast commemorating it, bestowed and continue to bestow on mankind. Since the birth of our Lord man has been confirmed in the hope with which he turns to God's throne for grace: God is on our side. But as I have said before this does not mean that God has dethroned himself any more than it means that man's life has been turned into a primrose path by that stupendous event.

We need to look critically at this tendency to sentimentalise the divine attributes by personifying them in the person of an innocent child or by over-beautifying the figure of the adult Jesus. The glamourising of the nativity story, the lowering of the whole tone of Christ's life to the level of a baroque sermon full of portentous warnings and grave moralisings has contributed quite a lot to western man's present helplessness in the face of conditions that keep him fettered and restrained. Certainly God became man, a man among men; but nevertheless God, master of all creation. Therefore man, the created being, must approach this God-made-man with reverence and adoration, subjugating himself in order to find himself – it is the only way.

The vigil points out how man ought to approach this feast. St Paul, in his epistle to the Romans, says this about his relationship to Christ: *for obedience to the faith in all nations.* Even allowing for the Pauline tendency to over-emphasise it is clear that every contact with God means prayer and response to a command. Whoever enters into the divine way of life automatically comes under the divine law. That, as far as the worshipper is concerned, means that the nearer he gets to God the more he yearns to return there for it is essentially a home-coming. God's nearness has dynamic power. The worshipper may know by the state of unrest into which he is thrown by this attraction just how much he has grasped of the secret relationship between God and man.

And the vigil further prevents our becoming bemused by the over-glamourised picture of the divine Child by pointing out another fundamental relationship between God and man. Suddenly and unexpectedly the collect reminds us that the Child, whose coming we so joyfully await, will be our future judge – in fact is already sitting in judgment over our lives. That someday the laughing eyes of the Child will harden with adult sternness, questioning and judging. The increased capacity for life which comes from heeding this warning, the awakened sense of responsibility, remains with us long after Christmas is over provided we have entered the vigil in the proper spirit. And if we remember that the divine Child of Christmas is already engaged in the serious business of judging the world how many of the people who represent the human race today can honestly approach the crib? Most of them don't even want to. The small and narrow door will not admit those who come riding on a high horse. But simple shepherds have no difficulty in getting through. The star leads the regal wise men to it but the arrogance of Jerusalem is thrown into a panic by the Child. How much there is in all our lives today that cannot face the Child. How different our individual lives would be if only we realised that the world's supreme hour struck that midnight when Almighty God condescended to come among us as a little child. We should not behave so greedily, so arrogantly, so high-handedly to one another if we did. Children do not strike to wound. But we pretend to be grown up and responsible; we are so proud and self-assured – and look at the result. The world lies in bomb dust and ruins round us.

Every hour of our Lord's life from the crib to the Cross by which we were redeemed is a judgment on some part of our existence. That is why we are so defeated and in such trouble. But his last hour was his resurrection, his glorious homecoming. We ought to take the Christ Child very seriously.

God whose coming we joyfully await is still the God of judgment. It is no easy or light matter to face the scrutiny of the divine Judge. The commandments alone make quite severe demands on us. And unwavering obedience to the Word which has to be the basis of our lives increases our responsibility. But even that is not the end. The laws are for the general ordering of life. Over and above them there are the entirely personal twists and turns of fate through which God intervenes in the lives of individuals. And so often he seems to leave us alone with our burden to cope with our troubles as best we can.

Let us re-read the gospel of the vigil from a human angle — looking at the episode in our Lady's life from a purely human point of view. We know how it all ended so it doesn't disturb us, but at the time there must have been a great deal of heart-ache. Joseph's belief in a trusted human being had been shattered — but what must Mary herself have gone through? She had dedicated herself to God — her submission was complete and unreserved. She had received the Word in a way no other human being would ever share. And then God became silent. She must have felt her husband's questioning eyes following her; she must have known the torment he was going through and the blow his sense of justice had received. And God left her alone in this hour with all the weight of her trouble pressing on her. From a purely human point of view what a terrible position to be in.

And what about our own fate? We have heard the promises and believed in the messages and accepted the prophecies. And then something unexpected happens and our life is twisted out of shape — human life is subject to that sort of thing, even the life of Christians. Ought it to be different in their case? — it isn't. And it is precisely when we come up against occurrences like these that our faith is put to the real test. To adhere steadfastly to the Word even when we strike our foot against a stone, even when we feel we are beaten, even when we are fastened in chains and handcuffs — that is the answer. And that is the answer that will be expected when each man is questioned at the seat of judgment; no one can escape it. God is posing that very question to us today in a hundred different ways and we have to see to it that we give the right answer. Steadfastness is not an easy virtue to acquire but it makes a man fit to face his Maker and it opens his eyes to actual reality of God.

Once a man honestly tries to acquire it the face of the whole world is changed. The stark features of unavoidable accident, of logical consequence and necessity are softened. The world, and life, take on a more friendly look – they seem to assume an almost parental compassion. The thousand and one small blessings which God takes delight in showering on mankind begin to reveal his nearness to us. Outwardly things are just as before and yet something has happened – there is a new consciousness of God's fatherly care in those who have stood the test of his questions. Suddenly man discovers that events are not impersonal and universal but that they have more than one meaning. In the personal dialogue between God and man which is the whole point of life, achievements have meanings quite different from those commonly attributed to them. And what one person regards as trivial everyday occurrences are to another blessed signs of God's mercy and guidance.

To breathe again. That brings us back to *respirare*, the deep breath of relief which can, and should bring ease. Nothing has happened to the world but it is now the ark of God which no storm can overturn, no flood can wreck. Life has not shaken off its laws or lost its tension but the Lord has subdued it, made sense of it all. The very tensions are harnessed now to increase the strength and the power of mankind.

And there is one other thing – man is no longer on his own. Monologue has never been able to make man's life happy and healthy; we are only genuinely alive when we are engaged in a dialogue. All mono-tendencies are evil. But by bringing the God-imposed tensions and burdens into the dialogue the most terrible of all human maladies – loneliness – is overcome. From that point there are no more starless nights, no more days of solitary confinement, no more lonely paths or pitfalls without companionship or guidance. God with us. That was the promise, that was what we prayed for and cried out for. In his own way, in the natural course of things, far more simply but also far more effectively than we could ever have imagined, God came to us as our ally.

We must not try to shirk the burdens he imposes on us. They are his way of communicating with us and they are his blessing. Whoever is true to life, however hard and barren it may be, will discover in himself fountains of very real refreshment. The world will give him more than he ever imagined possible. The silver threads of God's mystery will begin to sparkle visibly in everything round him and there will be a song in his heart. His burdens will turn to blessings because he recognises them as coming from God and welcomes them as such.

God becomes man but man does not become divine. The human order remains unchanged with the same obligations. But it has acquired a blessing and man has grown in stature, has become stronger, mightier. Let us trust in life because this night will pass and a new day will dawn. Let us trust in life because we do not have to live through it alone. God is with us.

IV THE PEOPLE OF CHRISTMAS

What is it that separates people from God?
Life with God and in God has its own laws and we cannot
discover what they are from a reference book. Yet the
conditions for their fulfilment are very straightforward
and clear cut – less obscure indeed than those of the ten
commandments. All the same the thin thread on which
they depend, the thread which unites the personal Thou
of God with the personal I of the created being, can only
be spun when they are being fulfilled.

The bridge linking the human with the divine has a
very definite architecture. Its foundations are God's affair.
In his all-embracing omnipotence he reaches out to
humanity in a thousand different ways. To penetrate his
mysteries, prayerfully and reverently to become aware of
him, is one of the highest exercises of the human mind
and we are most likely to find the key to his perpetual,
relentless, compassionate, gracious reaching-out towards
us in the lives of those whom we call saints. But the
pattern which he has set for his relationship with man is
not really my present concern. If that were my only pre-
occupation I should simply be satisfying a pious but very
ordinary curiosity in spite of the exalted subject. But in
order to get anywhere I must probe much more deeply,
as indeed I am trying to do. It is a question of the fundamental conditions a man must achieve in his own personal
life – what he has to do to draw the bow-string taut and
release the arrow so that the creative dialogue may begin.

I am not here casting the least doubt on the dogmatic teaching of the divine omnipotence and its good-will towards mankind. There is no hint of doubt of the operation of grace, of God's goodness or of the merit of good deeds and decisions by which man confirms his attitude towards his Maker. But within this framework man has certain liberties and responsibilities and these are the crux of the matter. It is here that mere curiosity is converted into existential thought about the mystery of the success – or failure – of one's life.

To take an example, how is it that the most eloquent, logical, well-prepared sermon may produce response in some and leave others unmoved? How is it that whole generations and periods can exist in complete ignorance of, or without response to, the idea of God's creative immanence as if they were incapable of receiving the divine impulse? How is it that there are people in all periods of history who remain unmoved by the greatest miracles, by the most convincing proofs of providential guidance, by the severest penances or the most inexorable strokes of divine justice?

Obviously this is more than merely an interesting theological or philosophical question – it is very pertinent to our fate today. It sums up everything and on the attitude we adopt to it depends whether we are going to place ourselves once again under the law of God's grace or whether, on the contrary, we are going to continue this miserable dance of death to the bitter end. It comes down to this – and there is no escape – to which order will man give his allegiance? Is he prepared to promote conditions in which the living contact with God can be re-established? For our lives today have become Godless to the point of complete vacuity. God is no longer with us in the conscious sense of the word. He is denied, ignored, excluded from every claim to have a part in our daily life. We have ceased to admit him to our lives, we behave as if we no longer need him and, what is worse, we have actually become incapable of being God-conscious. It is a terrible thing to say about this modern world but as far as I can see it is true. We don't even have to look very far for proof of it — there is sufficient evidence in the things that are happening every day and pious horror at the state of the world will not help us in any way. The law to which our lives are subject which has brought about this state of affairs has already made our existence a reproach, reduced the world to rubble and ashes, to carnage and destruction. Now our most urgent concern is how to overcome the inner misery and seal off the source of this external chaos.

Christmas is the mystery of contact with God, fundamentally and actually. Those who are part of the approach to it can show us the human requirements which will make it possible for man once more to converse with God, and the conditions necessary if we are to re-establish contact with him.

Three different kinds of approach are suggested by the Christmas mystery. First there is the historical sequence of events recalled by the feast; secondly there is the liturgical reconstruction of the mystery; and thirdly there is the silent, yet eloquent, participation of all present. Even the empty places have speech of their own and a message for us.

Those round the crib

We are familiar with the crib figures inside the stable or making their way to it. And on that journey to the stable they all have something significant to say to us about the mystery of life and the everyday world. Mary, Joseph, the angels, the shepherds, the wise men; these are the people gathered round the Child. Let us seek their message and learn their judgment on our own lives.

Mary. Let us put aside, for the moment, the venerated figure of the Blessed Virgin as such. It would be impossible to discuss that holy figure in one short paragraph; as our Lady she is a theme with an endless and perpetual message. But let us here think of her simply as the young girl, Mary, kneeling humbly before the manger in which lies the child she has just given us. She has her own message, a few words to offer us in the turmoil to which the estrangement between our benighted generation and the divine mystery has thrown us.

The fact that this night of nights brought forth the Light, that Mary kneels before the Child, that motherhood and the grace of compassion have become a law of our life, that the ice of man's inner solitude can be broken and melted by healing warmth – all this became possible only because the maid Mary yielded of her own free choice to the inner prompting of God's voice. Her secret is self-surrender and willing acceptance, offering herself to the point of complete obliteration of her personal will.

That is both her message and her judgment of us. As a generation we are completely wrapped up in ourselves; we are always concerned with *our* self-fulfilment, *our* self-realisation, *our* living conditions and so on. Everything is organised for our self-gratification. And precisely because of this we are getting progressively poorer and more miserable. Mary's decision was complete surrender to God and it is the only thing that can lead to human fulfilment. Hers is the decision that obeys the law of life.

Joseph. He is the man on the outskirts, standing in the shadows, silently waiting, there when wanted and always ready to help. He is the man in whose life God is constantly intervening with warnings and visions. Without complaint he allows his own plans to be set aside. His life is a succession of prophecies and dream-messages, of packing up and moving on. He is the man who dreams of setting up a quiet household, simply leading a decent home life and going about his everyday affairs, attending to his business and worshipping God and who, instead, is condemned to a life of wandering. Beset with doubts, heavy hearted and uneasy in his mind, his whole life disrupted, he has to take to the open road, to make his way through an unfriendly country finding no shelter but a miserable stable for those he holds most dear. He is the man who sets aside all thought of self and shoulders his responsibilities bravely – and obeys.

His message is willing obedience. He is the man who serves. It never enters his head to question God's commands; he makes all the necessary preparations and is ready when God's call comes. Willing, unquestioning service is the secret of his life. It is his message for us and his judgment of us. How proud and presumptuous and self-sufficient we are. We have crabbed and confined God within the pitiable limits of our obstinacy, our complacency, our opportunism, our mania for 'self expression'. We have given God – and with him everything that is noble and spiritual and holy – only the minimum of recognition, just as much as would serve to flatter our self-esteem and further our self-will. Just how wrong this is life itself has shown us since in consequence of our attitude we have come to abject bondage dominated by ruthless states which force the individual to sink his identity in the common mass and give his service whether he wishes or not. The prayer of St Paul – *do with me what thou wilt* – the quiet and willing readiness to serve of the man Joseph, could lead us to a truer and more genuine freedom.

The angels. Not the plaster images we have made of them but spirits of a higher order of existence identified with freedom, loyalty, wisdom and love. We meet them in the opening scene on the plain of Bethlehem singing hymns of joy and praise. But that is not the mystery or the law they represent – that is its fruit and reward. They bring tidings; they announce God's mystery and summon the listeners to the adoration from which they themselves have risen. Their mystery is that they represent the afterglow of the divine reality they proclaim.

That is their message and their judgment of us. For a long time now there have been no great spirits among us. They have dwindled and died out because gifted men have themselves broken the laws of the spirit. For the last hundred years intellectualism has been obsessed by the glorification of self, as if truth and reality ought to consider it an honour to be perceived and recognised by such marvellous individuals. Spirit is no longer regarded as the living reflection of a higher life. Perception and awareness now pose as spirit itself. Dozens of prophets kindle new lights each with his own message, his own ideas but with no notion of mission or dedication – that would be an offence against the autocracy and autonomy of genius. That is why for a very long time there have been no communications worth listening to. We have had no messengers of glad tidings singing paeans of praise. Whenever such a voice has been raised it has seemed illusory or has come from agonies of suffering – an indication of the depths of our soul sickness.

Adoration, perception, proclamation; this is the cycle that represents the life of the spirit. Adoration prepares the soul for perception since it loosens the tensions and dispels obstacles. The message once perceived enriches the soul, fulfilling its innermost needs and desires. But the proof is in the unfolding of life itself.

Let us return to praising God, to proclaiming him joyfully and then we shall find words that are significant and valuable. We shall see visions again and penetrate mysteries. Insight and decision and the message of the spirit will again become matters of importance, pushing aside the empty show and the bombast of 'presentation' which have so much influence nowadays.

The Shepherds. They are symbolic of a type. That they happened to be shepherds is unimportant – they might equally have been farmers or hedge-crawling tramps who spent their nights in the open. But they had to be men capable of registering wonder so I very much doubt whether they could have been products of this mechanical age. They had to be men whose hearts still warmed to the recollection of the old promises. Men, therefore, whose lives still had wide horizons from which the light of intuition and a thousand forebodings of spiritual realities were not excluded. Men still able to believe in miracles. Men upright and healthy enough to accept facts as facts even when their mathematical calculations and the results of their experiments pointed to the contrary. Their secret lay in their modest purity of heart, their lively wakefulness of soul, their instant readiness to respond to the call. And underneath all this lay the fact that their lives still held desire and expectation; they longed for the fulfilment of the promises they remembered and implicitly believed.

That is their message for us and the standard they judge us by. As a type men like these simple shepherds no longer exist. I am not referring to the profession or occupation but simply to the character of these men, to that wakeful readiness to accept miracles, that genuine inner prompting which altogether overshadowed self. The astonishing instinctive confidence which expects a miracle springs from the inner relationship between the yearning of mankind and the promises of God. This type is no longer with us. The world is full of miracles but no one perceives them; our eyes have lost the power to see. God's messengers would take a hand in our affairs more frequently if only our hearts could recapture the rhythm that calls them forth. Of all messages this is the most difficult to accept – we find it hard to believe that the man of active faith no longer exists. If we can revive faith in all its strength the whole world will change.

The wise men. Whether they were really kings or just local eastern chieftains or learned astronomers is not the least important. Their hearts were filled with wisdom and the aspirations of their race and that is what really concerns us. Only men of the highest type could have undertaken such a journey for such a purpose. They brought all the longing of their people with them to the place of the encounter for its fulfilment. Through the desert, by way of royal palaces, the libraries of the learned and the counsel chambers of the priests – and they ended their journey at last at a manger in a poor stable.

Here again we have a distinct type. The secret of these people is as plain as in the case of the shepherds. They are the men with clear eyes that probe things to their very depths. They have a real hunger and thirst for knowledge.

I know what that means now. They are capable of arriving at right decisions. They subordinate their lives to the end in view and they willingly journey to the ends of the earth in quest of knowledge, following a star, a sign, obeying an inner voice that would never have made itself heard but for their hunger and the intense alertness hunger produces. They believed in that voice more implicitly than they believed in the tangible realities of the mortal existence. Such men are regal in every impulse; they can rise above every situation even when it involves great suffering. The compelling earnestness of their quest, the unshakable persistence of their search, the royal grandeur of their dedication – these are their secrets.

And it is their message for us and their judgment of us. Why do so few ever see the star? Only because so few are looking for it. People often resolve to do things and then trivial, more pressing preoccupations get in the way. At the time of the nativity the world had already been under firm control for a thousand years. Everything was well organised and things were getting better every day! We have been saying this for so long nowadays that our middle-class complacency has become sated with banal truisms and at last is forcing us to ask a few questions. But we are still at the perplexed and puzzled and frustrated stage; we have not yet reached the point where these questions set up a sense of inner compulsion and urgency. The star which could light the way is still invisible to our half closed eyes.

What are we looking for anyway? And where will we find a genuine yearning so strong that neither fatigue, nor distance nor fear of the unknown nor loneliness nor ridicule will deter us? Only such a passionate desire can prompt the persistence which is content to kneel even when the ultimate goal turns out to be a simple stable. Men capable of such dedication penetrate to the heart of things and understand why that should be the outcome. A thousand secret longings of the spirit and the heart have paved the way for faith and sanctified them for the act of adoration.

Figures linked with the feast

So many figures come to mind when we are thinking about the feast of Christmas. All of them have a very special message for us. The innocents of Bethlehem even have a place in history. The others are so intimately associated with the mystery of contact which is the essence of this feast that they throw a penetrating light on our question and supply a valid answer. It is still the same question — how is the human soul prepared and fitted for this great encounter — and further, how can we help make it ready? What are the essential decisions of the heart for establishing a real and living contact with God?

St Stephen. His secret is easy to discern. He saw clearly that mankind had been lifted to a new plane through the miracle of the holy night and the encounter with Christ; that man now had new strength and the new responsibility of bearing witness. What had been enough before was enough no longer. Hence the expressions full of grace and strength — signs and wonders. But these things have not been given to man merely for him to master himself. Since Christmas God is with us and injustice and even murder are sanctified and transformed into signs of grace and strength and salvation. St Stephen's law is that of extraordinary self-surrender and extraordinary witness.

This is his message and his judgment. He challenges

us to get out of our rut. As we draw near to God the old and familiar become useless. God will transform us into faithful witnesses if we earnestly and with complete surrender turn to him for help.

St John. The very mention of that figure of glowing light conjures up many mysteries. We need only select three words which express the whole range of divine reality and at the same time sum up the character of the evangelist himself – light, truth and love.

These three words suffice both for the message and the judgment. Where today are those radiant souls whose light extends to eternity? Where are those whose ways are the ways of truth? 'The truth shall set you free' St John said. Today's bondage is the sign of our untruth and deception. So in these conditions let us take as our example those who have dedicated themselves to love. Seeking the light, living the truth and practising love will cure all our ills.

The holy innocents. The children of Bethlehem. They too have their place here. They share the scene with our Lord. And the mystery of the words 'all this happened – *because the Lord came,*' applies particularly to them. They were not martyred because of the power of a frightened and insane tyrant – that is made quite clear. And we see how completely all life is in the possession of our Lord. It is not mere pious sentiment to call the Child *kyrios.* Our concept of God must retain its grandeur and become firmer. Then the love we profess will also be strong, effective, reliable.

The mystery of the innocents is that they are the victims. The divine eagle gathered them as booty to himself. The blow aimed by the tyrant at our Lord fell on them instead. They serve as a kind of guard of honour to the divine Child – and the militant dialogue between God and anti-God in which they are caught up earns them heaven. But we have lost our awareness of that ceaseless duel – we so little realise that we have a share in the struggle that we ignore it completely. Yet no one can escape responsibility and at any moment God, exercising his sovereign power, may draw us into the thick of it. So far as an adult is concerned this can only lead to salvation if the victim voluntarily accepts the combat and enters it on God's side. But in the case of the innocents the manger sealed their fate and was sacrifice enough. That is their mystery.

And it is also their message and judgment. We have become insensitive to the sovereignty of God. Even where awareness of it still exists a clear cut concept of the relationship and of the order to which it belongs is lacking. The God under whose inexorable law we exist has been dissolved in a mist of psychological outpourings, subjective living conditions or collective existential needs. This is one of the worst evils of our time.

St Thomas of Canterbury. He too fits into the nativity picture. Here we have a man with a two-sided personality. He was chancellor and later archbishop – that is a man of authority living in the sphere of power, of palaces, of renown, a man of the purple. The mystery of St Thomas is on two different planes. When the chancellor became archbishop he was expected to subordinate the Church to the state. And the man who had been chancellor would probably have done so. But the office changed the man. He took the conditions of his new rank seriously. And this matter of the inherent order of things is vitally important. And it involves a second condition. Because of this inherent order Thomas sacrificed his life for God.

He died for the greatest Christian mystery, yielding his life for the sanctity of the Church.

His message and judgment are supremely important. The laws of order that govern this life are in no way inferior to the divine laws. Only those who submit to them with complete resignation can face judgment calmly. That is a message that should be taken to heart by a generation that has lost all sense of reverence and at the same time it is a measuring rod by which that generation must be judged. Untrammelled subjectivity is not the ultimate secret of being. A genuine contact must be established in which the partner, whether a thing or a person, is under no sort of compulsion either idealistic or material. The partner must have freedom to respond and speak for himself according to his nature, even to the point of being helped to speak his mind and express what he feels so that the dialogue may be truly reciprocal.

St Thomas's second message and judgment are closely linked with the first. The mystery of contact on the night of the nativity is not a subjective and lyrical romance. It embraces very clear ordinances of the Church. Oh I know well the Church often stands in its own light as well as in God's. But this is precisely where loyalty and steadfastness are called for. When all is said and done Bethlehem was no palace but a common stable. God lives in his laws. Since the clear duty of the Church is to conform and obey there can be no hope of finding God in disobedience. Whoever has fulfilled the duty of obedience has a right to cast a critical eye over the realities of the Church and where the Church fails the short-comings should not be glossed over. This is a matter of vital concern to intelligent and capable men who have truth and its fruitfulness at heart.

The people who are not at the crib

Even those who are not there have a message for us and a judgment to give if only to make us realise what it is that keeps us separated from God. After all as a race today we are not at the crib either. Yet the emotions aroused by all that we are living through ought certainly to make us want to be there.

Those who were not there include the powerful, the wealthy and the learned leaders of the synagogue, that is the heads of the established church.

The powerful. Neither the Roman procurator nor the recognised native rulers made their appearance at the crib to receive ratification of their power. Power can only be genuine and good when it is rooted in the divine. These people possessed power in their own right and used it only to further their own ends. Theirs is the mystery of power. Those who possess power have the implicit duty – and the opportunity – to serve as God's deputies. The French, more realistic than we are, have two different words, *force* and *puissance*. *Puissance* conveys the awe-inspiring impression of inner power. Power in itself and as the sum-total of all the means of enforcing it becomes destructive in the hands of arrogant totalitarian authority and ruins both the one who wields it and the subjects on whom he exercises it. The tyrant in possession of such power is no longer capable of spiritual sensitivity. He is suspicious of everything that does not fit into the narrow limits of permitted and regimented expression. There was no paragraph in the rules at Jerusalem covering the birth of the Child at Bethlehem. Hence the reaction of perplexity and fear and the prompt recourse to the sword. In circumstances like these the subject beings grow timid and cowardly; they accept that their claim to life is cut to the basic minimum of official permission.

Dare we ignore this message and judgment? The history of power in the western world is one long story of ruthless force. There is no room in it for the glory of God which is neither safeguarded nor respected. The great are concerned only with their own importance and spend their lives jockeying for position. And the consequences, as far as they concern mankind as a whole are only too obvious. Fear has become a cardinal virtue. This is not said in a spirit of anarchy. But power must regain its proper dimension allying itself with eternal purpose and genuine mission. Otherwise it will merely evoke counter-action and the ghastly struggle for survival will never end. And as a subordinate being man must waken to the inherent sovereignty of his spirit, believing in conscience and in his relationship with God.

The wealthy. There is nothing wrong in a man's having great possessions. But when his possessions rob him of his freedom and make him a slave then they become evil. It was like this at the time of the nativity and the palaces and fine houses were not destined to shelter the Lord. Great possessions can and should be a blessing. But the owners of treasure are also people who are afraid of any order of things not covered by the official records. It is so now and it was so then — our Lord's words on the subject are well known.

A great many hasty judgments have been made in this connection and much prejudice has been based on them — Marxist socialism, the condemnation of private ownership, and so on. We must keep a sense of proportion. All the same it is clear that the unsolved problem of wealth, of unearned income and so on is one of the themes of our time. In the last century control passed from the hands of great men and these burning questions no longer came up against the moderating influence of tolerance, wisdom and a sense of duty. Evils that were dealt with by the materialistic society of the nineteenth century were at the mercy of self-interest, expediency, indignation. The highest ideals were lacking and there was palpably no trace of that spiritual attitude based on the divine nature that makes all men free. So it is not surprising that the ordinary man's spiritual mechanism has rusted and become practically useless. Therefore those endowed with great possessions cannot be found in the devout circle round the crib. Some are absent because their possessions have robbed them of proper insight, others because the things they covet have made them incapable of any other interest. It is undeniable that every human being is entitled to living space, daily bread and the protection of the law as a common birthright; these are fundamentals and should not be handed out as an act of charity.

The learned. Learning and prayer have little in common. It was so then and it is still so today. Learning is besotted and bemused by the brilliance of its own ideas and has an overweeningly high opinion of its own interpretation of the world's affairs. And whenever the world takes a course not laid down in the books it is immediately suspect.

Western thought it inordinately proud of having 'grown up' in the last century. It considers itself completely adult and self-possessed. Meanwhile in obedience to its own law it is no longer spreading its wings like an eagle, no longer adventuring to the horizon. It has become a mere appendage to earth-bound utility blind and blunted to certain aspects of the truth. But human nature is so constituted that even in its most debased and blinded state it still needs to ape God and set itself on a pedestal as if it were divine. Unconsciously it is reaching out towards a state it might be capable of achieving if it were not so in love with itself and forever leading itself and its world into the icy mire of materialism.

No, the learned are certainly not found among those devout souls kneeling round the crib in the stable. They are the types whom later, when he had grown to manhood, the Child was to embrace in the lament 'Woe, woe'; but then they did not understand that either. The wise men, those whose prescience came from the heart, knew where they were going and the goal they were looking for. *They* were capable of adoration.

The learned today cannot be bothered with prayer. Should their thoughts ever wander in the direction of the crib they would surround it with signs and symbols, propaganda slogans, culture jargon and so on. They overlook the simple, unquestionable truths God has laid down. Clearly the whole destiny of the west is tied up with this problem. A glance into our schools and universities should suffice to prove that the problem of destiny is unsolved.

The established church. The synagogue had no part in the adoration at the manger. The synagogue in fact was one-track minded; it had an expectation and had no time or attention for anything except that clear-cut idea and its hoped-for realisation. The books had even foretold that Bethlehem was the place where that realisation would come to pass, yet so completely were the priests shrouded in their own shrivelled ideas that their senses had become numbed and that numbness prevented their recognising the signs of their time. No star pointed the way for them, no gleam of intuition lightened their darkness. They were bemused by their own self-sufficiency and heard nothing of the angels' song.

If only this were merely a tale to point a moral. But it is the plain truth; it really happened. The new spirit of Creation flows without interruption through the new Church – but how much force it requires to achieve its purpose. The officers of the Church have the inner guidance of the Spirit – but what about the executive departments? And the bureaucratic officials? And the mechanical 'believers' who 'believe' in everything, in every ceremony, every ritual – but know nothing whatever about the living God? One has to be very careful in formulating this thought, not from cowardice but because the subject is so awe-inspiring. One thinks of all the meaningless attitudes and gestures – in the name of God? No, in the name of habit, of tradition, custom, convenience, safety and even – let us be honest – in the name of middle-class respectability which is perhaps the very least suitable vehicle for the coming of the Holy Spirit.

The Spirit will go on pouring forth and bringing about its work of renewal but things might have worked more smoothly if there had been no rift, no quarrels, no secession, defamation and suspicion, if the Spirit had found living organs to work through instead of withered officials. And the obstacles are still there. Creative theology, spiritually conscious worshippers, active, effective love have yet to be achieved. Let us go back to the genuine contact and learn its laws once more; let us regain the capacity to see visions and know intuitively, moved by the Spirit. Let us give free rein to the divine instinct with which we are endowed and climb out of this morass in which we are bogged, emerge from this trance of false

security. Then we shall discover the real efficacy of
prayer and its power to bless and to heal.

The crux of the matter

Now I ought to sum all this up in a pattern of behaviour
towards which man could be educated so that he can be
capable of knowing God once more. But I am desperately
short of time. I can hear the gaoler already coming down
the passage and besides I have no more paper. So the
friend for whom these lines are intended, and any others
who may one day chance to read them, will have to
gather up the ends for themselves.

But one thing must be said. I shall be accused of being
concerned only with the 'natural' life of man. I will not
attempt to deny or disguise the fact. But *his kindness
appeared* in one of the Christmas messages. Without a
minimum of sound humanity, genuine human dignity
and human culture, no man is capable of making contact
with God. He is not even capable of ordinary understanding and behaviour.

I am perfectly aware that only extraordinary grace can
re-awaken man and heal him; I also know that the divine
impulse is forever prompting us, yearning to be allowed
to do its healing work. To proclaim this is the task of
those among us who still have perception and know it
for the truth.

For God will not deny his mercy is the law of our salvation.
But the main task is to render man capable and willing
for the Spirit to do its work. This is even more urgent
than the proclamation of the central mystery for no one
can understand this anyway until he has surrendered and
opened his heart to the will of God within him. So it may
be that even this shambles in which we now live, this

devastation swept by bitter winds of fate, is the destined place and hour of a new holy night, a new birth for humanity seeking God, a new nativity. Darkness shall not frighten us or distress wear us out; we will go on waiting, watching and praying until the star rises.

V EPIPHANY 1945

It may be possible to find an hour to think today. How many things there are to think about and what contrasts they present. The feast itself with its rich symbolism; the emergency of God from the quiet corner of Bethlehem into the wider world; the guiding star; the men who have braved the wilderness; the joy of the encounter; the terror-stricken king; the indifferent clergy; the wonderful providence of God. And besides all this, all the other things the feast commemorates – the baptism in Jordan, the hearing of the Father's voice, the marriage feast of Cana. So very much to turn over in one's mind.

Then the personal aspect. The many years I have spent. in preparation and the day for renewing my holy vows This year, in this time when men are yearning for a star to guide them and not a glimmer of a star appears because men's eyes are blind and cannot see, the message of the feast is more than usually urgent. We must pass it on and stir people's understanding.

But to come back to my own personal predicament; in two more days my case will come up for trial. Just two days in which I can rely only upon God for there is no other help I can turn to. How I have prayed for a Christmas star, for light on this problem. But God has left it unanswered; he is asking me to make the 'step to freedom' – the decisive stride which will carry me from myself to lose myself completely in him. Here also is a wilderness to be crossed and a terrified ruler only too eager to use the sword.

How can I best sum this up, make a mental picture which will unravel my perplexity? Situated as I am I should so love to be able to give my friends (and myself) one word whose genuineness would be unquestionable because it had been won from God himself. But up to now I have not found that word. Will the last hour eventually produce it for me? I realise now as never before that a life is wasted if it cannot be summed up in one word, one direction, one ruling passion. Only a human being who has this secret can rise to his full stature; everything else is mass-produced, subject to any conditions others choose to impose. And the hall-marked individuals are rarely met with nowadays – that is why life lacks purpose and makes so little sense. The genuine dialogue no longer exists because there are no genuine partners to engage in it. People are frightened, they are scared to stride out firmly and honestly to the boundaries of their potential powers because they are afraid of what they will find at the border line. The man who aims at fulfilment only within the framework of his own limitations must always be afraid of the unknown. The existence of the limitless, the eternal that is beyond our comprehension and yet vaguely draws us as being within our capacity for experience is the real source of our uneasiness. It is precisely here that man's judgment and assessment of values comes in.

For the man who desires to develop his highest potentialities today's feast gives the laws and conditions which should regulate his life. It shows him the way by which he can achieve a real proved individuality.

The law of freedom

Man needs freedom. As a slave, fettered and confined he is bound to deteriorate. We have spent a great deal of thought and time on external freedom; we have made serious efforts to secure our personal liberty and yet we have lost it again and again. The worst thing is that eventually man comes to accept the state of bondage – it becomes habitual and he hardly notices it. The most abject slaves can be made to believe that the condition in which they are held is actually freedom.

During these long weeks of confinement I have learned by personal experience that a man is truly lost, is the victim of circumstances and oppression only when he is incapable of a great inner sense of depth and freedom. Anyone whose natural element is not an atmosphere of freedom, unassailable and unshakable whatever force may be put on it, is already lost; but such a man is not really a human being any more; he is merely an object, a number, a voting paper. And the inner freedom can only be attained if we have discovered the means of widening our own horizons. We must progress and grow, we must mount above our own limitations. It can be done; the driving force is the inner urge to conquer whose very existence shows that man's nature is fundamentally designed for this expansion. A rebel, after all, can be trained to be a decent citizen, but an idler and a dreamer is a hopeless proposition.

Man's freedom is born in the moment of his contact with God. It is really unimportant whether God forces man out of his limits by the sheer distress of much suffering, coaxes him with visions of beauty and truth, or pricks him into action by the endless hunger and thirst for righteousness that possess his soul. What really matters is the fact that man is called and he must be sufficiently awake to hear the call.

The law of freedom is an appropriate theme for today. When those worshippers knelt in homage on the floor of the humble stable with everything else put behind them – their homes, the wilderness, the guiding star, the agony of the silent star, the palace of the king and the grandeur of the city – when all these had lost their value and their impressiveness and the worshippers' whole being was concentrated in the single act of adoration, the symbolic gesture of laying gifts before the manger signified the achievement of liberty. Then they were free.

Man must leave himself behind if he hopes to have even a glimpse of his true potentialities. But this surrender of self is the thing we find most difficult to accomplish and so rarely succeed in. To the modern mind it makes no sense because we have lost any concept of the boundless glory, the shimmering, unlimited wonder of the divine to which we gain access by yielding up our own limited personality. Only when we trim our sails to the eternal winds do we begin to understand the sort of journey we are capable of undertaking. Only by voluntary unreserved surrender to God can we find our home. Any other sort of refuge is only a temporary shelter, a poor hovel on shifting sand destined eventually to fall in ruins. Adoration in a stable is preferable to terror before a throne. There is much wisdom in the ancient teaching about the passing of the soul because it embodies the idea that man can only become himself by stepping outside himself. Pray and praise are the two key words to human liberty. The kneeling attitude with outstretched hands is the correct attitude for a free man.

Our age, like those before us, has tried many other ways. But the life-urge is very strong in any man of genuine feeling and it keeps forcing him back to his own potentialities. We found it very hard to let go of beautiful things. But in the end we had to. We came to the stable by a road which was laborious, terrifying and blood-soaked and this miserable dwelling was at the end of it. Our hands are empty — more than empty. They are torn and bleeding because things literally had to be wrenched from their grasp. But if in spite of everything we can hear and recognise the call, if we can discover the inner meaning of the grim experience through which we are passing and if in the midst of this frightfulness we can learn to pray, then this hell will bring forth a new man and a blessed hour will strike for the troubled earth in the middle of the night — as it has so often before.

The fate of mankind, my own fate, the verdict awaiting me, the significance of the feast, can all be summed up in the sentence *surrender thyself to God and thou shalt find thyself again*. Others have you in their power now; they torture and frighten you, hound you from pillar to post. But the inner law of freedom sings that no death can kill us; life is eternal. *Pray and praise* — the fundamental words of life, the steep roads to God, the doors that lead to fulfilment, the ways that lead a man to his true self.

The law of the wilderness

Those for whom the hour of freedom struck in the stable at Bethlehem had faced and overcome the wilderness, both the external wilderness of isolation, forsaken home-land, lost relationships and friendships of a momentous and strenuous pilgrimage, and the inner wilderness of uncertainty, doubt, fear and anxiety. It had been a long and a weary journey and their faces still bore the marks of the hours of strain even in the glow of the blissful encounter. The wilderness has its proper place in the drama. Human freedom is the fruit of liberation, of the persistent and tireless scaling of the enemy fortifications.

When children kneel before the crib lisping *adoro* and *suscipe* their prayer is valid – but more is expected of an adult. He must master the real meaning of the words and gestures or go back and learn his lessons over again. Human freedom is the result of a tough and painful liberation; healing and happiness are not imposed on mankind and life is not a lottery with colossal prizes.

The wilderness is part of it all, the wilderness of the soul as well as the body. One could write a whole history about wildernesses. All really great men have had to fight against loneliness and isolation and the great fundamental questions that occur to a man in such circumstances. The fact that our Lord retired into the wilderness shows how genuinely he took to heart the laws and problems of humanity. And then, after the trial of the wilderness had been withstood there will still be the temptations to be met. Great issues affecting mankind always have to be decided in the wilderness, in uninterrupted isolation and unbroken silence. They hold a meaning and a blessing these great, silent, empty spaces that bring a man face to face with reality.

There are no more profitable places in history than wildernesses – vast areas – the sea, high mountains, trackless forests, plain and pampas and steppe, barren land as well as fruitful, all exercise their own peculiar influence, not only on the physical being but even more on the dispositions and characters of the human beings affected by them. They all leave their mark on history. And of all wildernesses the streets of great cities – deserts of stone – are unique in that again and again they have ended up as the graveyard of history. The wilderness concerns all humanity, all its actions and decisions, in a very special way.

Any life that cannot measure up to the wilderness, or seeks to evade it, is not worth much. There must be periods of withdrawal alternating with periods of activity and companionship or the horizons will shrink and life lose its savour. Unless a man consciously retires within himself to that quiet place where he may think out great problems he cannot hope to solve them and if he denies himself this healing effort an evil fate will certainly overtake him. God, who loves him, will chain him in loneliness, perhaps to his own undoing.

And the world too will be in a bad way if ever it happens that there are no more wildernesses, no more silent unspoilt places to which a man can retire and think, if every corner of the earth is filled with noise and underground tunnels and soaring aeroplanes and communication networks, if cables and sewers scar the surface and undermine the crust. Mankind needs to keep a few quiet corners for those who seek a respite and feel the urge to retreat for a while from over-civilisation to creative silence. For those who occasionally feel the hermit instinct there should at least be a chance to try it out. The law of absolute utility, of total functionalism, is not a law of life. There is an extraordinarily close connection between the wilderness and fruitful, satisfying life. Where all the secluded places ring with tumult, where the silent muses have been degraded to pack-horses and all the sources of inspiration forced into the service of official mills grinding out propaganda, the wilderness has indeed been conquered –

but at what a price. Even greater devastation has taken its place.

The wilderness has a necessary function in life. 'Abandonment' one of my friends called it and the word is very apt. Abandonment to wind and weather and day and night and all the intervening hours. And abandonment to the silence of God, the greatest abandonment of all. The virtue that thrives most on it – patience – is the most necessary of all virtues that spring from the heart – and the Spirit.

Please don't think I am trying to write an ode to the wilderness. Anyone who has ever had to encounter and withstand a wilderness must have a healthy respect for it – and must speak of it with the reserve that prompts a man to hide his wounds and his weaknesses. It is a great place for thinking things out, for recognising facts, for getting new light on problems and for reaching decisions. A heavy load brings the ship low in the water but it also keeps her steady. The wilderness represents the law of endurance, the firmness that makes a man. It is the quiet corner reserved for tears, prayers for help, humiliations, terror. But it is a part of life and to try to avoid it only postpones the trial.

The law of grace

However the wilderness is neither the beginning nor the end. In his perilous climb to the heights of freedom man is not entirely dependent on his own resources. The more he has to overcome, the greater the distance he has to travel, to transcend himself and find his true self, the less he can depend on his own unaided power. Both as a race and as individuals we have experienced and discovered how miserably inadequate our own feeble efforts are.

97

Please God it may be a long time before we again over-rate our personal powers in so devastating a fashion.

Freedom is born in the hour of contact. And it is not as if God simply stood there, waiting for the weary traveller to arrive. Both God and man are travelling towards one another. God shows in hundreds of ways his willingness to meet man more than half-way – to put out his hand when man tends to stumble. And this is not the full extent of his divine aid – this is merely the preliminary. The summit is reached when man hears his voice; then he can no longer doubt that his destiny is to rise above himself to his fulfilment.

Today's feast uses three symbols for the divine attraction that draws man with gifts of grace – the star, the sacred river, and the water changed into wine. But they are only symbols, not the truth itself. For the star signifies the Child, the river signifies the Lord and the divine remission and forgiveness of sin, and the wedding feast signifies the coming of the Spirit for our salvation. Humanity is made to see that it is not only under the law that demands grace but it is also under the law of genuine and effective grace. Precisely where he most needs help man finds it because God has placed himself on an equal footing with us. We are not alone – we can face anything that befalls us. And more than that, we are capable of living effectively when everything in our world seems to be against us. Remember St Paul said: 'My grace is sufficient' – and it was sufficient to such an extent that to this day the world still admits it. Another great man said: 'God alone suffices' – and he did suffice for a life whose fruits the world is still reaping.

At the present time we are still wandering in the wilderness. The cry for help still rises from our hearts. It is true as far as we are all concerned and it is true for me personally. In this situation the wilderness has lost its peaceful appeal and assumed its more threatening aspect hinting at unknown dangers. This is no figure of speech but actual fact. We nine are acutely aware of the great community, the world of men ranged against us, and we are the 'lost ones' who tomorrow have to start on an unknown journey to meet our fate.

But the wilderness will not lead us to final doom but to a great freedom. The wilderness exists to be overcome. And I know that I am not alone. The law of truth and love and prayer still holds good. I must let the healing current run its course so that the waters of bitterness will be turned into the wine of divine blessing; *pray and praise*.

THE TASKS IN FRONT OF US

I THE FUTURE OF MAN

God-conscious humanism

Every meditation on humanism is historically handicap-
ped at the outset. There has already been a humanism – in
fact there have been several. And unless the humanism of
the future succeeds in cutting itself off completely from
its predecessors it is hardly likely to inspire confidence.
And quite rightly. But it is not easy to establish that we
are dealing with true humanism and at the same time
overcome, or rather transform, the versions that have
gone before.

The essential requirement is that man must wake up
to the truth about himself. He must rouse his consciousness of his own worth and dignity, of the divine and
human potentialities within himself and at the same time
he must master the undisciplined passions and forces
which, in his name and by bemusing him with delight in
his own ego, have made him what he is. This is not a
disparagement of passions. Woe to the man who tries to
live without any – that is the way to disintegration. Man
must take himself as he is with all the undercurrents and
the fire of his nature. But the destructive element in
passions, the element which knows neither limit nor
restraint, must be brought under control or it will tear
man to pieces and destroy him. Man's passionate pre-
occupation with self must be subordinated; he must
retain all the strength and fire of devoted human love but

without the blindness, the irresponsibility, the lack of instinct that makes it destructive.

Man wants to be happy and it is right that he should. But by thinking only in terms of self man destroys himself for it is a limited concept and has no room for anything stronger than the human order. Left entirely to himself man is unhappy and intrinsically insincere. He needs other people to give him a sense of completeness; he needs the community. He needs the world and the duty of serving it. He needs eternity, or rather he needs the eternal, the infinite. And there we come to the new, God-conscious humanism.

The lessons of history

In my study of history I have been constantly filled with regret that we only hear of things after they have already happened. We ought to be able to arrange matters so that we could shape our own history. That would save mankind much distress and suffering. As things are the road through history is often a way of the cross.

Men who make history are swayed by conditions as they find them, by the dynamics of situations and by the rhythm of their own individual characters. These can affect trivial and unimportant matters and they can also affect whole states, bringing decisions as to the fate of nations down to the narrowest personal level.

Such decisions which condition the actual pattern of any given period are dictated sometimes by intuition, by mood, by fancy or by wishful thinking; sometimes too by expediency, by necessary defence measures which force many detours and false starts on the historical subjects before they can arrive at their predestined consummation.

Every age and nation has its mission in history. And the sooner they realise this, and set about fulfilling their role the quicker they will escape from history's ruthlessness to a state of comparative peace. But the problem is always to discover the right theme for a given nation and a given period. A great many people – the majority in fact – never get beyond the stage of viewing life from the historical standpoint as a perpetual struggle for the bare necessities of existence. Life to them is a workroom for the exploitation of subjective passions or for labour in the service of the great 'I'. So it is important that every nation should have a few individuals capable of perceiving universal tendencies and of making them known again and again. Even Plato wished that philosophers were kings. We are in just such a situation today. My own opinion is that it offers possibilities and responsibilities for Christians. It is not a major task but it is still a function the Christian is capable of performing if he takes his purpose in life seriously because he knows of the supernatural influence on history.

The bitter lessons man has learned from experience in the past hundred years ought not to be erased by chaotic events or a way of life that has again become primitive. These things should be thought out and the results handed on to act as a guide in future trials. It is impossible for me at this moment to arrange the experiences and results in either hierarchic or logical order. I can only put down a few points that seem important to me. The tasks in front of us are:

1. An 'existence minimum' consisting of sufficient living space, stable law and order and adequate nourishment, is indispensable. The 'socialism of the minimum' is not the last word on the subject but the essential first

word, the start. No faith, no education, no government, no science, no art, no wisdom will help mankind if the unfailing certainty of the minimum is lacking.

2. A minimum of honesty in every field is equally necessary.

3. A minimum of personal standards and human solidarity is necessary.

4. There must be a minimum of world wide dedication and sense of service. Any idea or ideal the age calls forth, even if it is only the shadow of absolute truth, is preferable to mass-minded thoughtlessness since it keeps alive in man a certain feeling for spiritual values without which his receiving apparatus for the spark of truth ceases to function.

5. A minimum of transcendence is essential – man must have something to look up to, to reach for, some kind of aspiration, if he is to be a man at all.

6. In addition to these minimum essentials there must be qualities to which man's desire can be wakened, which he can feel himself capable of attaining.

All this is the 'existence minimum' that I would like to sum up in the words respect, awe, devotion, love, freedom, law – the words which, in my opinion, represent genuine fulfilment.

And in conclusion the 'existence minimum' will only work if all the essentials are co-ordinated to work in harmony with each other. Individually this adds up to character; collectively it means the family, the community, the economy . . .

II THE EDUCATION OF MAN

To return to my familiar theme, that man today is profoundly Godless. This is a basic fact affecting both his judgment and his decisions. But it also goes even deeper than that for modern man is no longer *capable* of knowing God. The great task in the education of the present and future generations is to restore man to a state of fitness for God and religion.

What actually does the present state of things amount to? It means that certain human organs have become atrophied and no longer function normally. And also that the structure and the constitution of human life today put such a strain on humanity that man is no longer able to express his true nature. This applies on the technical-sociological plane as well as on the moral plane. Hence man has built up in his own mind a picture of himself as a sensitive animal with mind, reason, temperament depending on circumstance.

We have to ask ourselves very seriously what has brought this state of affairs about. We cannot, for instance, lay all the blame on the last few decades. They are the harvest but the seed was sown much earlier. Reading Goethe – particularly *Dichting & Wahrheit* and *Wilhelm Meister* – one cannot help noticing signs that modern man was even then well on the way. The centre of gravity had already begun to slip. He indicated the different processes of development of which present day man is the end-product. There is the inner development resulting from this shifting of the human centre of gravity which has its own inescapable logic and consequences. And there is the external development represented by the technical, sociological, scientific and industrial world. These developments have influenced and furthered each other. Present day man is in the strictest sense both the product and the slave of the world in which he lives. But that world has become what it is because of the breakdown of the inner standard which should have controlled man's choice and safeguarded his ability to master the conditions in which he lives.

And what now? Three possibilities suggest themselves. First we must preach the divine order and centre our hopes on it. Secondly we must restore human order and await a general improvement as a result. And thirdly we must bring order to the chaos of man's living conditions and then trust to the emergence of a new man.

But if I preach till I am black in the face, trying with whatever skill I may possess to persuade man to resume his proper status yet as long as human beings have to exist in inhuman and unworthy conditions the majority will succumb to them and nothing will make them either pray or think. Nothing short of a complete change of the conditions of life will have the least effect. The revolution of the twentieth century has need of an ultimate aim; it ought to be to guarantee every human being space to grow in.

But even if this happens under a democratic constitution, if things are left in the charge of present day man then sooner or later they will degenerate into chaos again. For present day man is sick and incapable of handling his affairs – he can no longer cope with life. So a new approach is necessary, a more intensive method. Man must be shown how to help himself; he must be spiritually and physically strengthened in order to rise to full stature. This involves education towards self-reliance, responsibility, judgment, conscience; education that will instil good-neighbourliness and eliminate the countless forms of superficial thinking and mass-mindedness; education towards transcendence, purposeful education towards perfect manhood, education towards God. All these things are intimately connected and you cannot have one without the others. Only a man with a certain spiritual awareness, however small, is fit to accept the word of God and fulfil the divine order in his everyday life. For no order can be achieved except in accordance with God's law. The new order of the world must be based on the historical fulfilment of the order of God, otherwise it will be just another edifice on shifting sand doomed to destruction like the rest. Man's regeneration must come from within according to the pattern which defines him as being created in God's image. Otherwise history will repeat itself and we shall be faced with further madness and confusion.

But how are we to set about it? It is obvious that all these things are important and linked – but where are we to begin? What is the first requirement, the essential foundation?

There will always be a few men who see things as a whole, aware of all the connections and implications, who can trace the truth in every outward manifestation to its roots, to that source where all things are linked by God and sustained by him. Such men must immerse themselves in two aspects of being – in the recognition and acknowledgment of God, that is to say in religion, and in the recognition and acknowledgment of the laws that apply to man's existence, that is to say in humanity itself.

Actually these two requirements need not be bracketed together. The man of great holiness is not necessarily an adept in worldly affairs. But if a saint should by chance be mixed up in worldly affairs they would inevitably start moving in the right direction for the mission of the saint, to render exceptional homage to God, is by no means opposed to the ideal order of things in this world.

All the same specialisation is fashionable nowadays and absolute thoroughness in both spheres is necessary. Religion in the past has often occupied itself so little with the practical problems of everyday life that it has been discredited, and worldly wisdom has so often over-reached itself that it has lost confidence in its own power.

Re-education and re-inspiration of the people will help to restore religion to its proper state of prestige and for that reason both are necessary. Anything that can help to heal man's spiritual ills or improve the conditions of his life should be encouraged even if it cannot solve the whole problem. Man must be induced to take himself seriously as a being created with a divine purpose to a divine pattern. He must be taught to recognise that pattern and to understand that it is his duty to realise it (existential humanism). Then through a sense of responsibility this humanism must be nursed and broadened into a new humanism, a God-conscious humanism.

But can this be described as the education of the individual to God? Let us start with the basic necessities. First the need to bring about conditions which will no longer require an almost superhuman effort on man's part to turn his attention to God. Then the need for conditions in which the human heart is healed, even as far as its desires are concerned, quickened by that holy yearning which only finds true satisfaction in God and therefore turns to God again. And most important of all, conditions which encourage a human being who is God-like, filled with divine power to address and challenge others.

In my opinion all the direct religious effort of the present time falls short as far as any permanent effects are concerned. As long as man lies bleeding, beaten and robbed by the wayside, the man who tends and helps him will be the one who wins his heart – not the one who passes by on the other side on the way to his holy offices because the man doesn't concern him. Therefore fuller and deeper religious teaching is needed for those who already have the genuine kernel of religious knowledge in them. They must be equipped so that they can go to the rescue of the rest of humanity and cope with the task of healing them. Man must be educated to resume his proper status of manhood and religion must be taught intensively by truly religious teachers. The profession has fallen into disrepute and it will have to be re-established. For the next few years those chosen to teach should be truly religious men ready to co-operate in all efforts for the betterment of mankind and human order. They should insist authoritatively on these efforts and not be satisfied with the mediocre.

In insisting on these I feel I am condemning present day religious endeavours as sterile because they do not help man in the depths of need but merely skim the surface. But it is how I see it – for instance none of the contemporary religious movements take as their starting point the position of mankind as human beings. They really concentrate on the difficulties of the religious minded man who still has religious leanings. They do not succeed in co-ordinating the forms of religion with a state of existence that no longer accepts its values.

Equally efforts directed towards bettering man's physical or spiritual existence ought not be made in order to acquire power. For the next few centuries Europe is hardly likely to tolerate alliances between altars and any kind of throne. The effort must be brought down to the level of the outcast lying by the wayside; he is the one who must be restored to human dignity by the release of his latent virtues and all the inherent good in his nature. Our concern must be with a man's reverence, devotion, love; only when he is using these capacities is he a man at all. We must direct our efforts towards re-awakening love. When this has been achieved man will begin to feel at home for a while and then the restless Spirit will lead him on to further progress.

III THE FATE OF THE CHURCHES

In future years the fate of the churches will not be decided by whatever their prelates and leaders can produce in the way of skill, wisdom, diplomatic talent and so on. Nor will it depend on the important positions their members attain. That kind of achievement belongs to the past. For the sake of their very existence the churches must somehow break away from their sentimentalism and outmoded liberalism. They must get back to fundamentals. Hierarchy is essential for genuine order and direction; the Church at least should know this by its own origin. But order and direction are not to be confused with formalism and feudalism. The hierarchy must make it plain not only that it is aware of the errors and foolishness of individuals but also that it is also conscious of the despair and yearning of the age, of the unrest of contemporary trends and that it can hear and answer the bewildered, frightened seekers who cannot find their way. Man must feel that the concerns of the modern age and the problems of the new generations are not simply filed away as records but are matters of active and urgent concern to those who have assumed the task of dealing with them.

A Church that makes demands in the name of a peremptory God no longer carries weight in a world of changing values. The new generation is separated from the clear conclusions of our traditional theology by a great mountain of boredom and disillusion thrown up by past experience. We have destroyed man's confidence in us by the way we live. We cannot expect two thousand years of history to be unmixed blessing and recommendation — history can be a handicap too. But recently the man turning to the Church for enlightenment has all too often found only a tired man to receive him — a man who then had the dishonesty to hide his fatigue under pious words and fervent gestures. At some future date the honest historian will have some bitter things to say about the contribution made by the churches to the creation of the mass-mind, of collectivism, dictatorships and so on.

Whether the Church once again finds its own way to the heart of modern man depends on two things. The first is so obvious that it can hardly need elaborating. If the churches persist in presenting humanity with the spectacle of a Christendom at logger-heads with itself they might as well give up. It is no use saying we should resign ourselves to the rift as a historical legacy, a thing we must bear like a cross. That impresses nobody nowadays. It is to *our* eternal reproach that we were not capable of preserving the heritage of Christ intact.

The second essential is the return of the Church to the service of man in a way that conforms to man's needs, not to private tastes or to the code of a privileged clergy. The Son of Man came to serve . . . By this standard the realities of many religious institutions would be found wanting. No man will believe our message of salvation unless we work ourselves to the bone, physically, socially, economically or otherwise, in the service of ailing humanity. Modern man is sick; perhaps I shall be able in the next few days to write down some thoughts on this sickness. Modern man has become an expert in many departments of life — his range of power is enormous. But he is intoxicated by his own cleverness and he has not yet realised all the sacrifices that have had to be made, how much has had to be given in exchange for this power. These things have not yet forced themselves on his attention – and it is pointless to try to keep reminding him of them. A wise guide keeps an account but tactfully refrains from producing it until the proper moment comes. Modern man, that worldly wise person who thinks he knows all the answers, is extremely sensitive to any form of presumption, real or imagined. And the precision which the scientific age imposes on many people makes them highly critical of the superficial way in which we churchmen often perform our duty in the wider sense of the word.

I said we must get back to the ideal of service. By that I mean meeting the man in the street on his own ground, in all circumstances, with a view to helping him to master them. That means walking by his side, accompanying him even into the depths of degradation and misery. 'Go forth' our Lord said – not 'sit and wait for someone to come to you'. There is no sense in preparing a fine sermon while we are losing contact with the listeners and leaving them to their fate. I look on the spiritual encounter as a dialogue, not a monologue or an address, a monotonous drone of words.

But all this will only be understood and desired when the Church again produces men who are in themselves properly fulfilled. Fulness; the word had a special attraction for St Paul. It applies today even more forcibly than it did then. Fulfilled men – not pious caricatures. Men who are genuinely impregnated with the spirit of their calling, men who have prayed with all sincerity: *make my heart like thine*. Whether the Church will again produce such fulfilled, creative men we do not know. But only if she does so will those she sends forth feel sufficiently secure to dispense with insistence on rights, sufficiently self reliant to relax the perpetual pre-occupation with traditions and so on. Only then will they see God's requirements with clear eyes even in the darkest hours. Only then will their willing hearts beat with a compassion that sweeps aside as negligible the old stubborn attachment to being 'right after all'. Their hearts will beat with one desire – to help and heal in God's name.

But how can we get to that stage? Churchmen seem to stand in their own light because of the habits they have acquired, historically speaking. Personally I believe that unless we voluntarily stride out across new ground, leaving the well-worn paths, history-in-the-making will destroy us with a thunderbolt of judgment. And that applies both to the personal destiny of the individual churchman and to religious institutions as a whole. Despite all right thinking and orthodox belief we have arrived at a dead end. The Christian idea is no longer one of the leading and formative ideas today. The plundered human victim lies bleeding by the wayside – must it be a stranger that comes to the rescue? It seems to me we ought to think about this very seriously. The burden that is pressing on the Church at the present time and disturbing it so much is man himself – the man outside whom we cannot find a way to reach because he has no longer any belief, and the man inside who no longer believes in himself because he has experienced and given too little love. All this should make us see that it is no use making fine speeches about reform or drawing up reform programmes. We ought to devote our energies to the development of the Christian character, preparing ourselves to *deal* with the needs of mankind, helping and healing in this age of unfathomable distress.

116

Most of the ordained in the official Church must realise for themselves that at present the Church is a misunderstood – and incomprehensible – reality to contemporary man and must be aware how disturbing, threatening and dangerous a state of affairs this is. We are going along two parallel roads and no bridge links them. Further we have both encouraged the belief that each is constantly sitting in judgment on the other. So far as the Church is concerned she has much to answer for. We ought to start with an honest examination as to how this state of affairs came about. And this probe must be free from any tendency to blame our opponents. And at this point of course up crops the old question – what good could such an examination achieve? Well first in importance is the recognition of the need for promoting respect for others. We must abandon our arrogant pretensions to reverence as a right. The Church must come to look upon herself far more as a sacrament, as a way and a means, not as a goal and an end in itself. Nowadays personal regeneration and revitalisation is far more important than even the most comprehensive factual knowledge. In sober honesty we must face the fact that the Church today is no longer one of the controlling powers in human affairs. And that it cannot be made comparable with any other powerful historical factor (alliance of throne and altar in any form) but its influence must be centred in the integration of inner life with human potentialities (*puissance*, not *force*). And the impact made by the Church's message on this plane depends upon the sincerity of its transcendental surrender and devotion. Arrogance anywhere near the Church is objectionable – and never more so when it occurs in the name of the Church, or worse, actually as part of the Church herself.

MAKING READY

I THE OUR FATHER

On this ultimate peak of existence at which I have arrived many ordinary words seem to have lost the meaning they used to have for me and I have now come to see them in quite a different sense. Some I don't even care to use at all any more; they belong to the past which already is far away. Here I am, on the edge of my cliff, waiting for the thrust that will send me over. In this solitude time has grown wings – angels' wings; I can almost sense the soft current as they cleave the air, keeping their distance because of the immense height. And the noises from below are softened and quietened – I hear them rather as the distant murmur of a stream tossing and tumbling in a narrow gorge. And the cliff edge is too narrow, movement is too constricted for real assessment and analysis. All along intuitively I have had the impression of frustration through restraint. Up here the only words that keep their validity and take on even deeper meaning are the words of the old prayers and particularly the prayer our Lord himself taught us.

Father
The word Father sounds strange in these surroundings. But it is constantly in my mind. Even in that ugly little room filled with hatred where men were making a travesty of justice, it never left me. In the past few months I have met nothing but hatred, enmity, pride and presumption from the people with whom I have been thrown into

contact; nothing but ruthless force intoxicated with its own autocratic power and usurped dominion. It would be a terrible thing if the grace-less life, to which today we are all subjected in one form or another, were the final revelation of reality. All we can do is to remember faithfully that God does call himself our Father, that we are bidden to call on him by that name and to know him as such — and that this pompous, self-important world in which we live is only the foreground to the centre of reality which so many scarcely notice in the noise and tumult surrounding them. The fundamental motif of our life is compassion and paternal guidance. Man has produced so many mad ideas to account for his condition — fate, environment, heredity, the world as the ultimate end of everything. Up here in this rarefied atmosphere it all sounds like the bleating of a lot of silly sheep pretending to be men — the words are not worthy of men.

God as Father, as source, as guide, as comforter; these are the inner resources with which a man can withstand the mass assault of the world. And this is no mere figure of speech — it is actual fact. The man of faith is aware of the solicitude, the compassion, the deep-seated support of providence in innumerable silent ways even when he is attacked from all sides and the outlook seems hopeless. God offers words full of wonderful comfort and encouragement; he has ways of dealing with the most desperate situations. All things have a purpose and they help again and again to bring us back to our Father.

Our Father

One of the most terrifying weapons in the hands of ruthless authority is enforced solitary confinement. It is still so even now we are all condemned to the same sentence and only await its execution. We never see each other — the whispered words of fellow-sufferers and friends are denied us on this last painful journey. We have come to the end of all things where man is utterly on his own. And the old truism, it is not good for man to be alone, applies especially to this situation and this dark hour. I would so love to shout across to another cliff where a friend sits equally isolated. But the words do not carry — they are caught up in this thin air where sounds do not travel. But then — *our* Father — and all at once the chasm is spanned. Suddenly we see the truth that in God, through God, we have always possessed the shortest route to reach our neighbour. Man knows himself to be at one with all who pray and believe and love. The common centre, the personal God who speaks to us, and to whom we speak, makes mankind human and the community a genuine whole.

Who art in heaven

The reality that lies beyond our earthly experience is often distorted and obscured. In this age we have almost ceased to think about it. Thus we have obliged God to make us very painfully aware of the temporal and impermanent nature of existence. The realisation often comes as a brutal shock. Even those of us who believe in the future life share the worldly view of the rest to some extent. Yet a man is only a man in so far as he respects the laws of his being in relation to his *whole* existence. Only such a man is capable of the true attitude, the proper approach, the reverence, the devoted love, the absolute obedience due to the Creator. We can only arrive at our true nature by lifting our eyes to the hills. It is because we have failed to do this that we are such mass-products, so 'typed', so incapable of coping with life – really incapable of recognising the fundamental principles and intuitions that belong to the man created in God's image.

Nor is it enough to have ideas or an ideal – much more is needed. The idealist is certainly more of a man than the purely earth-bound, materialist individual who has no time for anything except 'facts'. But complete fulfilment and realisation can never come from idealism alone. The inner crust is unbroken – untouched and sterile. A man only becomes a man in the inner fastness of his own personal *I am*. And unless the dialogue takes place this inner identity slowly congeals and freezes to death. Man cannot dispense with the dialogue; he needs it so that he may grow and fulfil himself. And the dialogue with the Absolute is of paramount importance, something far beyond a mere idea or ideal. The God of life is a personal God and only when man enters into the dialogue with him does he begin to realise his dreams. In this conversation he learns the fundamental principles of his being – adoration, veneration, love, trust. Anything undertaken on a plane lower than this dialogue, no matter how much zeal and sincerity and devotion go into it, is in the end incomplete. Adoration is the road that leads man to himself.

The realm of the personal God is heaven, that is to say it is the sum-total of all that man considers to be his life's greatest happiness. Fulfilment and more. It is not primarily a place or a period in time or anything like that. It is fundamentally God himself – a conscious union with him. Anyone who has achieved that union is in heaven. It is a union that uproots all our limitations and destroys our previous habits if we are fortunate enough to begin to experience it here on earth. The records of the world's great mystics that have come down to us witness this. But for most of us the breaking up of our present form of our existence, that is our death, is the usual gateway to God. On that plane things merge into each other; the things a man loves or longs for, happiness, joy, heaven, and the things he reverently praises, God and his fulness are brought to one focus.

Love of heavenly things is something the Church often prays for as the summit of grace and fulfilment. It is important to throw a bridge across to fulfilment, to the future, to that which is hoped for not only as far as the desires of our nature go but also as far as our attitude and conscious effort are concerned. We must aim at heaven with all our strength. Man will have to re-learn, much more positively and intensively than before, that life leads from the personal dialogue with God to the actual personal encounter and the experience of unity with God. He will have to learn that this is his heaven and his real, his only, home. Then he will learn to pray, not merely as a duty and in obedience, but with intense vitality and with all the driving force of his own free will.

Hallowed be thy name

The images evoked by the Lord's prayer vividly illustrate man's life. Man, humanity, stands or falls by the things that are mentioned in it. If this is realised we can begin to make progress. If it is not realised, or not taken seriously, we sink and decline. That is the real key to the grim picture of life today. And this phrase, *hallowed be thy name*, teaches man to pray for the worthy ideal, for the unassailable, holy, venerated standard. Unless they have something of supreme value, something at the centre of their being which they can venerate, human beings gradually deteriorate. Human nature is so constituted that it must have something holy that it can worship, otherwise it becomes cramped and distorted and instead of a holy object of veneration something else will take its place. I ought to know for I have just emerged from a murderous dialogue with such a self-appointed object of veneration. These substitute values are far more autocratic and demanding than the living God himself. They have no idea of courtesy or of waiting for their turn, or of the blissful encounter, of voluntary persuasion, of gracious appeal. All they know is demand, compulsion, force, threats and liquidation. And woe to anyone who does not conform.

The word of God should evoke and receive the great veneration this phrase suggests, praise, reverence, awe. This effects the realisation of those fundamental categories of life I referred to just now. The name of God is the holy of holies, the central silence, the thing that above all others calls for humble approach. Man not only ought to believe in the truth at the centre of his being, in the purpose of his existence, but he should also bear testimony to this belief by the proper fulfilment of his life's purpose. He should subjugate everything to this law of holiness and reject everything that does not harmonise with it. God, the great object of man's veneration, will then also be his whole life. 'There is no healing in any other name.' How little there is to say once we have said this. And how much that is said is mere cant. We have so many pious phrases that are utterly without genuine reverence for God. Religious chastity and silence go well together.

Let us resume the practice of giving names to life and to things. I have been a mere number long enough to know what it means to be nameless and what effect it has on life. As long as life itself has no name, or at least none that it honours, men and things will continue to lose their identity in the dreadful regimentation and anonymity into which we have sunk. Life has a sensitive nervous system through which everything is connected. Since the name of God is no longer the first and foremost of all names in the land and the voice of the people, then everything else that was once precious and prized has lost its name and been subjected to false and falsifying labels. The cliché, the label, the uniform, the slogan, the 'dominant trend of the masses' – these are our rulers. And pity the man who dares to differ, to proclaim his own thoughts or use his own name.

Prayer is our way to freedom and education in the method of prayer is the most valuable service that can be given to mankind. It makes it possible for the temple and the altar to occupy again their rightful place and for humanity to humble itself and measure its responsibilities in the name of God.

Thy kingdom come

Man has permanent need of supernatural power and strength. If his communication with the divine is stopped he begins to have strange dreams and set up false gods – success, people, new orders and so on. I know this only too well. I have dreamed and yearned and loved and laboured and it has all added up to a hymn of longing for something final and permanent. No man can get much further with his dreams and ideals – he keeps coming up against his own limitations and the insufficiency of his creative efforts. This, too, I have proved for myself. I know how often one discovers one is playing with shards while dreaming of shapely vessels full to the brim, and how the heroic song we set out to sing so often dwindles into a plaintive whimper. Man, left to himself, can accomplish nothing. And the purpose of this part of the prayer is precisely to make man realise that he needs supernatural help and that all the power of the living God is at his disposal. I have proved this too – proved that a man can be instantly lifted out of his own inadequacy to the point where no harm can touch him and where he is and remains equal to anything even when things turn out very differently from what he had expected. The genuine dialogue becomes part of him.

The kingdom of God is where man is in a state of grace and all things move in divine order. Human needs are met by God's abundance, human limitations are dissolved by God's power, human rashness is tamed by God's discipline – all this is part of the kingdom of God. It is a quickening in man's innermost heart, passing from man to man. It is a silent grace which nevertheless gives impetus to word and deed; it exists both as an action and an order. Everything that we need today is covered by this prayer. Contact with God is the one thing that gives sense and satisfaction to our lives and God is always ready and waiting – waiting with benificent readiness, not tyrannical coercion. The kingdom of God is grace, which is why we pray for it; but the grace of God so often stands at the door and knocks without finding anyone to open.

Man raises a barrier between himself and God's kingdom in two ways – first by the kind of life he chooses to lead and secondly by his demand for certain social conditions or his toleration of others.

But the absolute minimum is alertness and willingness to receive. In himself, as a purely human and natural being, man is graceless and his course through life graceless and unmerciful. In the long run his progress through life is destructive both for himself and others. Despite his Promethean outpourings he is at the mercy of things and quite unequal to the tasks and problems he is faced with. That is the clue to the history of recent times where none of the pressing problems have been successfully met. If man cannot bring himself to turn completely to God he must at least consent to be receptive so that God can reach him. This prayer stipulates repentance on man's part, and his consent to a revolution – that is a willingness to uphold a social re-organisation that will enable him once more to open his heart to God and thus become ready for the contact. The most pious prayer can become a blasphemy if he who offers it tolerates or helps to further conditions which are fatal to mankind, which render him unacceptable to God or weaken his spiritual, moral or religious sense. This prayer asks a great deal of God – no less than himself. But at the same time it imposes a great responsibility on man. Whether it is really offered as prayer or whether it is mere pious cant depends on the way in which man accepts and carries out that responsibility.

Thy will be done on earth as it is in heaven
This is man's prayer for freedom. It may not sound like it but it is so all the same. Man is a being set on a certain course. Any attempt to evade that course, to ignore it, set it aside or destroy it must inevitably lead to disaster. The very fact that he constantly has to take into account factors over which he has no control makes him cautious. He keeps coming up against circumstances which impose all kinds of restraints on him, from polite considerations of tact and good manners to actual duty and obedience.

Even on this level any pretence to self-sufficiency means self-deception, delusion, suicide. There is no creative 'splendid isolation'. And this is even more true on the plane of man's supernatural obligations. God has a place in the definition of man both as *God from whom* and as *God to whom and by whom*. Any other concept man may form of himself is disastrous and likely to be fatal.

The link with God binds man to his order, his law — which is the reflection of his nature. It is a link with his freedom, his mysterious grandeur. These are the things a man must reckon with if he wants to remain a man. God's order binds him both because it is an integral part of the natural structure of human existence and also as a point of contact with the requirements of the law. God's freedom lifts him beyond all this into the wider sphere of personal submission, vocation, trials, visitations and so on. Man's greatness and worth — that which raises him above the average — is decided in this personal dialogue with the exacting God. But God's might, his hidden mystery, brings man up against obscure ways, dark visions, brilliant revelations, the mystery of the supernatural which cannot be put into words.

Only in voluntary acceptance of all this will man find freedom. Failing such acceptance he is a slave to his fears and the things he would like to hold on to. He must cut himself adrift and leave all things behind if he ever hopes to find his true self. Until he has made complete severance he cannot experience this blessing — and once he has experienced it he will know it for a foretaste of heaven. The will of God in heaven is the ratification of God by God and the confirmation of God by the blessed. Self-acknowledgment and self-confirmation make the great jubilation of the Trinity, the torrential life of God. And the confirmation of God by those who have reached fulfilment is the substance of their fulfilment – they are caught up in the divine jubilation and blissful torrent of divine life. And of course the will of God, which is to be done, is always and fundamentally good will, healing will. The surrender, the encounter with God's freedom and God's mystery mean contact with salvation.

Give us this day our daily bread

We can accept this petition as it stands, at its face value. It has been coupled with the words of our Lord 'My meat and drink is to do the will of my Father' and it has been held to refer to the holy eucharist. These are pious reflections but here I am concerned with the prayer's literal reference to the recurrent hunger of humanity and the bread which is meant to satisfy it. The Lord's prayer teaches us to bring the perplexities of our everyday lives to God and talk them over with him. The affairs of the 'earth' are now to be considered – bread, trespasses, struggle, evil. The things that occupy and trouble us in our daily lives are very real. Our Lord has taught man how to pray. Man's cares and man's blessing are the contents of the Lord's prayer.

Man's daily bread really is God's concern: lack of bread and prayer for bread are part of man's make-up and the prayer acknowledges these two fundamental factors. Philosophers have summed up one in the words *basis of life* as though they regarded it as an essential but altogether inferior necessity. Intellectual people often have that kind of snobbery. Of course one can idolise bread and make a god of one's stomach. But if one has endured hunger for weeks on end it is a very different matter. Anyone who has ever undergone such a trial knows that an unexpected crust of bread can seem like a real gift from heaven. I can vouch for this because I have personally experienced it. Only one who has known the effect hunger can have on every life impulse can appreciate the respect in which bread is held and what the perpetual struggle for daily bread really means. We will preach in vain about the kingdom of heaven, or even the kingdom on earth, as long as men go hungry and daily bread is something that must be struggled for. Bread always was one of the greatest mediums of temptation and still is so. Nothing can be more important than placing the problem of distribution of bread in the right hands. And the bread problem must always be a subject for prayer, otherwise man will lose himself in the material world. No matter how abundant and dependable it may be bread still comes day by day from the eternal provider and man must realise this. Such truths and their implications must be kept transparently clear, or the consequences are dangerous.

That is why we are not enjoined to pray for overflowing barns and well-filled store houses; we are only told to pray for daily bread. The hazards and uncertainty of human life find an echo here, and the fact that life justifies itself in trust rather than in security. Anxiety regarding income, insurance, pensions, dividends and so on has been responsible for much destruction in recent years. We who are enduring a second war in these days of 'welfare' and for the second time experiencing a bread-shortage know what it means. Bread is important. Freedom is even more important. But most important of all is unshaken loyalty and adoration without betrayal.

132

Forgive us our trespasses as we forgive them . . .
It is as natural for man to err as it is for him to need daily bread. Our urgent need for bread is not more real than are our faults. I am not referring here to original sin, that burden we have inherited from the first catastrophe at the dawn of creation. That is also a fact but it has been over-emphasised so that it has produced only an echo. This underlining of original sin has led man to adopt two different attitudes — one because the natural strength of which he is conscious belies the fatigue and incapacity with which he has been credited. Some do not understand — and others pretend not to understand — that the incapacity refers to the supernatural order and its fulfilment. The scandalous revolt against God that we have witnessed in the western world has robbed this thought of most of its force. The second attitude is utter indifference to failure since man is told that he cannot act otherwise. To regard sin not merely as a lapse but as a personal reproach and responsibility has become completely foreign to western mentality.

But I mean precisely this when I say that sin is part of our daily life. We fall into sin because we give up and fail. We are guilty in the fact that we are living in a given moment of history and we have allowed things to happen which are a reproach to us. There is such a thing as a personal attitude towards God and there is also a public attitude, that adopted by the community as a whole. Our generation is guilty, grievously guilty. It is very important that this should be acknowledged. This guilt must be washed away, we must be absolved from it — otherwise we shall perish. Man performs strange dances round his sin but instead of being rhythmic his movements look like epileptic contortions. Man can try to escape from his guilt – that is forgivable because it is a natural reaction. He can try to deny it, he can dream in the manner of the ancient Greeks and try to argue it away. All this helps to blind his eyes and stifle his conscience – but the guilt remains. Deeds that have been committed are like endorsed cheques – sooner or later they are bound to be presented. Man can only gain remission of sin by repentance. He must recognise and acknowledge that sin inflicts a wound on God's creation, a wound that defies all the arts and strength of creative being. As a sinner his only hope lies in turning to the healing forgiveness of God. This generation urgently needs men prepared to stand before God for its sins.

God bids men place their hope of mercy in the mercy they are prepared to show. The sins of the world must vanish with transcendental guilt so that the world now and then may breathe again. As far as we are concerned this means that we must refrain from all bitterness against those who have wronged us. I bear them no grudge; I forgive even that charlatan who made such a travesty of German justice. They even arouse my pity. But I pity still more the people who have delivered themselves and their holy spirit into the hands of such monsters. God help us.

Lead us not into temptation

We ought to offer this prayer very seriously. Our Lord knew what it was to be tempted and what bitter struggles temptation may entail. Who can be sure of himself? When things are going well we let these words pass over us negligently, thinking very little about them as if they really did not apply to us at all. And then all of a sudden the sky becomes overcast – a storm arises, and with the wind blowing from all directions at once we do not know which way to turn. Take this journey of mine up the perilous face of my cliff. How many hours of weakness and despair have had to be endured in making that climb, hours of sheer helplessness, of doubt, not knowing which was the best course. How is it that conditions suddenly get distorted, their balance disturbed and their threads twisted and entangled producing a pattern far from our intention and quite beyond our power to unravel? No one can escape the hour of temptation. It is only in that hour that man begins to sense his weakness and to have a faint inkling of the vital decisions he is expected to make. If only I can manage to keep a hold on this perilous perch and not faint and let go.

I have committed my soul to God and I rely on the help of my friends.

Temptation assails us from within and without. Compulsion, force, pain, humiliation, one's own cowardice, God's silence, complete inability to cope with an external situation, all these call for painful decisions. And added to all these there is fear, that creeping worm that eats its way into a man's very substance. The devil within may break loose – indignation, doubt, the overwhelming wish to live which cannot be suppressed. All these can cause many hours of bitter struggle and when it dies down the world no longer seems the same place. One's skin is turned to leather, criss-crossed with scars and wounds.

We have only God to fall back on in such a moment. This, and the knowledge that we have not brought the temptations upon ourselves voluntarily are our only hope. God bids us pray that we may be spared such trials. I advise everyone to take this admonition seriously to heart. What a witches' cauldron my own experience has been. How it will end, what still awaits me sitting here on the brink of the precipice, and how long I shall have to stay here before I must take the plunge, I have no idea. Nor do I know for certain that the gnawing worm within may not become active again. We must guard against every kind of false security – only then will we find access to God's great peace and omnipotence. How very different my feelings were during those hours in court. Then, although I knew from the start that I was doomed, I had no real sense of defeat. That was thanks to divine strength. And life from that moment took on a new meaning. It was clear and unmistakable that life is worth living and worth dying for. If this is true it applies in the fullest measure to moments of temptation when man cannot depend on his own strength alone.

Deliver us from evil

This part of the prayer again applies to man involved in temptation. Resistance is not only a manifestation but a thing that weighs the outcome in the balance. We are under a strain and begin to doubt whether we shall find salvation. In temptation it is a question of deciding for or against God and the essence of temptation is that it robs our judgment of its clear-cut certainty in making decisions. No one can escape deciding for God but the danger of making the wrong decision is a thing a man must pray to be spared. And incidentally this prayer requires far more humility and honesty than are usual nowadays.

The evil from which we pray to be delivered is not that which is most oppressive in life, such as poverty, worries, hardship, burdens, sacrifices, pain, injustice, tyranny and so on; it is the chain of circumstance that leads us into temptation, disturbing the balance, pushing life off-centre, distorting the perspective. It will be seen at once that the so-called 'good things' of life are just as liable to cause such disturbance as the painful and hard realities. These things all possess the potential power to lead or force us into temptation and by that I mean all the things that can possibly come between us and God.

Life is a contest, and this is emphasised by the words 'deliver us from evil'. The passage is even more eloquent than the one preceding it. In the natural course of existence we are again and again brought up against both the agony in the Garden and the temptation of the wilderness. There, too, genuine temptation had to be met, because our Lord was weak with hunger and because the devil found him vulnerable. The devil. Yes there is not only evil in this world, there is also the evil one; not only a principle of negation but also a tough and formidable anti-Christ. Man should give thought to the fact that he must distinguish between the spirits. And to the fact that wherever self is stressed, as in strength that glories in its own might, power that idolises itself, life that aims at 'fulfilling itself' in its own way and by its own resources, in all these, not the truth, but the negation of truth may be suspected. And there is only one thing a man can really do about it – fall down on his knees and pray. Only after ten long years – ten years too late – do I fully realise this.

II COME HOLY GHOST

The Holy Ghost is the breath of creation. As in the beginning the Spirit of God moved on the face of the waters, so now – but in a much closer and more intimate way – God's Spirit reaches the heart of man bringing him the capacity to grow to his fulfilment.

Theologically this is clear – the heart of grace is the Holy Ghost. That which makes us like Christ is the same indwelling Spirit – the principle of supernatural life in him and in us. Believing and hoping and loving, the heart beats of the supernatural life, are the created being's participation in the self-affirmation of God which is expressed in the Holy Ghost.

The cry of 'come' can be interpreted in this way. It embodies the intensified hungry Advent-yearning. It is the will to break through barriers, to escape from fetters and confinement.

And send from heaven

From heaven – out of this world, of God's reality. From that place where all things are united in one, not scattered over the earth. The created being must cry out to some power beyond itself in order to acquire its share of strength; when man realises and acknowledges that his natural powers on their own are inadequate he has taken the first step towards salvation. He needs the mission and the assignment God gives him, the permanent guidance and healing of God if he is to meet the forces of destiny

138

on equal terms. And as man is a being limited in form and capacity by the set pattern to which he is created, and does not exist by his own strength and power, so too his potentialities are a free gift and a grace. Man has always tended to forget this ever since the beginning of time – he always tends to fall in love with his own estimate of himself. We all proceed from one failure to another and after every collapse we come out with less substance and more wounds – all of us. When we are tired and tempted to give up, instead of blaming fate and circumstances we should ask ourselves whether we are living sufficiently close to God, whether we have called on him earnestly enough. Help comes from the hills – and they are here, at hand; their help is simply waiting for us to apply for it. My life at this moment should prove this. Everything points to the fact that God has chosen this way to teach me this lesson. All that I was so sure of in my self-satisfied judgment and so-called wisdom has been shattered by the experiences and the disillusionment I have gone through. *God alone suffices*. These last few months have blown a great deal of my work sky high; according to the verdict perhaps my very existence on this earth must come to an end. Yet there have been miracles. God has taken my case entirely into his hands. I have learnt how to send up my cry and to wait for the message of encouragement from the eternal hills.

Send thy radiant light
Light is symbolic of one of the great longings of human life. Again and again we find ourselves benighted, sunk in deep gloom, without light to guide us. How could we even desire light if it were not for the eternal gift of grace which gives our spirit a vague intuition that dark-

ness is not its natural and final state, that even in the darkest hour there is something to be hoped for, a state of fulfilment towards which the spirit must aspire. God created man as a light-endowed, radiant being, and as such sent him forth into the world; but we have blinded ourselves to this truth. Only a faint inkling of it remains. Man is never more soul-sick than when he becomes confused and finds himself helpless to cope with a situation. That is the primary meaning of this prayer – it is a despairing cry for divine help to dispel our self-imposed, sinful darkness, wiping the dreams and the fear from our eyes so that they may see again. But there is also another imperative need for light in our lives; God's radiance dazzles us. We get presentiments and glimpses but they are transitory and usually lead nowhere. Men who are dedicated and prepared pray for divine light which will heighten their perception and raise them to realisation of that fulness they have hitherto only dimly guessed at. Once a man has arrived at this stage he knows what the strength of God is even in the darkest and most hopeless situations of his life. When life becomes most serious our own ideas always wither or become childish. This has been proved again and again in our individual lives and in the life of the community.

Come thou father of the poor
Three times there is this cry of 'come' breaking from the depths of human misery and helplessness to the comforting presence of God. This cry is the arc that connects the created being with the Creator's divine fulness. In it the two realities meet in a simple and fundamental relationship. Man recognises himself as a pitiful creature incapable of satisfying even his most pressing needs by his

own effort – and that is the key: man wants to live and intends to live but does not possess the wherewithal for living. This applies to every part of life even in the middle of abundant material riches. One of our Lord's beatitudes refers to the poor in spirit. Yet the overcoming of need is the promise made to those who have it and it applies to all those who are still held in bondage by their need, whatever it is. How often I have sent up these three cries of 'come' during these weeks of hunger – they have become my grace before meals.

To the man in need God's Spirit appears fatherly, that is as all-providing strength and power directed by love. That is as it should be. When man acknowledges his need, presenting himself without vanity, self-assurance and so on in all his naked helplessness, God manifests himself in miracles of love and pity. The effects may range from the ease of heart-ache and spiritual illumination to the satisfying of physical hunger and thirst. When we send up this cry we call upon the Spirit of creation. We are desperately poor; let us acknowledge our poverty and offer up our prayer for ourselves and our race.

Come bounteous giver

Three times the 'poor soul' sends up its cry to the Creator and three times the healing, omnipotent Father hears that prayer. It is good for the soul to persist in its pleading. The Holy Ghost is the Spirit of fulfilment, inner strength, infinite abundance; it is the Spirit of fulfilment in its divine essence. God comes to the summit of expression in the Holy Ghost; all the passionate adherence of God to himself is affirmed and confirmed by the third Person of the Trinity. His law and divine order is really summed up here – what is unfinished must be completed, fulfilled; and that fulfilment is the Holy Ghost. *Bounteous giver*. Again I say the Holy Ghost is the breath of creation, the mighty current which would like to gather everything up and rush back to its original source. The soul which is weary and sick and conscious of its poverty should call on the Holy Ghost. He is the giver; through him we can be shaped to the likeness of the Son. He gives us new life and makes us capable of living. He heartens us, strengthens our will, heightens our understanding so that we may believe and hope and love – that is so that we may draw nearer to God and live in unity with him. And he is the giver of gifts in the narrower, often forgotten, sense – the seven gifts of the Holy Ghost. These bring man new potentialities, enable him to live more abundantly. Our supernatural life is genuine life and therefore it is differentiated and the more faculties a man is able to quicken the more fully he will live. Everything grows and becomes more efficient under the creative blessing of the *bounteous giver*. Human misery and need are things to be overcome and all this is very relevant to the problem. Nietzsche's declarations and his dreams concerning superman eventually depress and bore us – indeed in the end they seem despicable. There is only one way to progress and that is by praying, and praying in the right way. In my present situation what help can I get from a concept of the greatness to which man should attain – what use is that in this isolation and loneliness? But to feel the warm presence of the Spirit, to be aware of his strengthening breath does help me along this lonely road. When we remember that we can call on God as the bounteous giver, *dator munerum*, the dispenser of blessings and strength, then adverse circumstances lose their power. The Holy Spirit finds ways and means to

give us comfort; he has resources of tenderness and
attention far exceeding the arts of human love.

Come light of our hearts

Once again we find God symbolised by light – it occurs
again and again. And the wonderful words 'light of our
hearts' indicate that we are here concerned with the
Spirit of God in the very centre of life, bringing healing
to its roots and its source. Man doesn't live and feel with
his thoughts – nor does he suffer through them until they
develop into a passion or become a burden to his heart.
Perplexity of heart is the greatest of all confusions man
can fall into and the extent to which his heart is committed is the measure of a man. In other words he is
measured by his ability to love. That is the key to a man's
personal life and also to history – it solves many riddles if
we realise that the history of mankind is the history of
human passions. And the history of human folly is the
history of unenlightened hearts. Man's risk lies in the
fact that he can become confused and irresponsible,
lacking sound instinct and good judgment, at that very
centre of his being where decisions are made. It is his
great misfortune that his instinct so often fails him. The
heart is the innermost core of man where all his capacities,
wishes, needs, and longings are concentrated and find
expression as decisions, impulses, love and surrender. So
here, in the very centre of man's being, the temple of the
Holy Ghost should be established. It is the nature of the
Holy Spirit to penetrate and blend with the life impulses,
purifying and completing them and thus imbuing them
with its own intensity and assurance. *Light of heart*. We
cannot pray for it too often or be too earnest in our plea
that our hearts may keep their harmonious rhythm and

143

their power of right feeling. Feeling is here the operative word – statement and explanation are of minor importance; feeling and instinct are the things that count. When the heart is in the right place, as they say, everything is in order. May the Holy Spirit have pity on this poor, foolish, hungry, frozen, lonely and forsaken heart and fill it with the warm assurance of its presence.

Best comforter

Comforter. We ought to take this word in its simplest and most straightforward sense. To be comfortless is a state of mind and spirit that results from misery experienced and recognised as a condition, a fact, particularly if it is one's own. Therefore there can be no comfort in a facile denial of the comfortless condition. There can be no comfort until things are changed and the new conditions are those the spirit can rejoice in and be satisfied with. For the essence of comfort is that the mind and spirit are no longer troubled, that they are in a state of security, order and fulfilment. The genuine comforter must either establish this new state or so harmonise the old state with existing circumstances that the misery vanishes and the whole situation takes on a new character. Both depend entirely on the action of the Spirit in us. The *bounteous giver* and *father of the poor* overcome inherent human misery and the *light of our hearts* makes us aware of the change that is taking place. Through the power of this Spirit we are armed to meet and overcome our moments of despair. We have only to keep on believing and praying.

Sweet guest of souls

The verses that follow describe the various consolations

bestowed on mankind by the Spirit of God. God does not dole out blessings one at a time. He is comfort and comforter. *Guest of souls;* actually present and present in a singularly personal way. True mystical experience is nothing less than the shatteringly conscious awareness of this continuous presence. The Spirit of God is the supreme comforter because it overcomes finally and absolutely the fundamental sensations of misery and helplessness by driving the poison out of them.

And, in spite of the necessary submission on the part of the creature, the whole of religion is a truly personal relationship and of nothing is this more true than of the divine intimacy between Creator and worshipper. It is an intimacy, a true friendship. The prayer refers to the presence of the divine friend as *dulcis,* sweet. We feel a bit embarrassed by the word in this connection. So many words have lost their original spiritual meaning and come down to us coloured by human emotion instead of spiritual experience. Let us admit frankly that this word, like most with a deep religious meaning, has been taken from this sphere of human emotional life. All great and fundamental spiritual feelings are inter-related and belong to the same class. The sad thing is that nowadays neither love nor religion have any real bearing on the words used to express intense bliss or inexpressible intimacy. Both as worshippers and as people capable of love we have deteriorated sadly.

Sweet refreshment

This phrase can only be really appreciated by those fortunate enough to know one of those people whose very presence is so infective that it makes him a source of strength, security, joy and trust, so inspiring that it changes the whole atmosphere, dominating it. The spiritual joy and inspiration conveyed by *dulce* radiate like heat – the air becomes warm and friendly. *Refrigerium* means melting, dissolving – what warmth and shelter are to the wounded who have suffered exposure, the comfort of the Holy Spirit is to the soul; only the soul, being more sensitive, feels this far more acutely than the body.

Rest in labour

These three prayers are the cry of the tormented soul yearning for contact with the healing strength of spirit. Here are man's three fundamental needs which are provided for by the current of divine healing.

The first need is: *in labore* – 'by the sweat of his brow' was the way it was put at the beginning. And out of this has grown the harassed, hunted man of today, totally enslaved to duty, never free from care, restless, hag-ridden. Duty, necessity, danger give him no respite from their imperative demands. And on top of all this are his personal difficulties – his anxiety for those he loves. This is what our life has come to. *In labore* – ceaseless strain, insecurity, helplessness – not knowing the answer to any of it. We have lost the freedom for which we were created and condemned ourselves to perpetual bondage and fatigue.

And this titanic drama of man's destiny is being played out on a stage that embraces the whole of humanity. Recent epochs decreed that *homo sapiens, homo speculativus, homo religiosus* and so on should be exterminated and replaced by *homo faber*. Now *homo faber* has arrived. Factories are the new cathedrals, machines are the magic symbols of today and man is the most easily convertible currency in this utilitarian world of machinery. Everyone has been drawn into this new order and none can escape its dictatorship. Life has opened a machine gun fire of demands on us and we cannot long withstand the onslaught – unless help comes from the hills. Unless man turns to that inner strength that lets him rise above all the trials that beset him. Only from within can we draw the calm that will lift us above the hectic rat-race even when we fulfil its demands and carry out our duties. Spirit has a way of adapting itself to man's needs, entering completely into his life and giving relief just where the need is most pressing. Where it is heaviest the burden will be lightened and where help is most needed it will be most vividly experienced. The Holy Spirit will give us the great virtue of perseverance. With his help we shall prove stronger than the forces ranged against us, swifter than the hounds of care that pursue us in this desperate hunt our lives have become. He will give us quiet assurance and silent fulfilment to enable us to endure. And though we may often think we have reached the end of our resources a new demand will find us not only ready but, in God's name, capable and willing to meet it. The one indispensable condition is that we remain receptive listening for the inner voice, otherwise we shall be drawn up in the sterile and stifling world of everyday realities. God's Spirit will pour itself through our every need, drown every noise, overcome all fatigue if only we will turn to it in faith and with desire. That is why our prayer today must be to the Creator Spirit, he who works in us and fulfils our needs bringing us to our true selves in our personal lives.

This very day, this moment in which our heart is crushed by weariness and our strength seems to have ebbed away, precisely now in the middle of all this trouble we pray for the healing peace of God; *in labore requies*. All you tired people who are battling under strain and sorrow that threaten to undermine your loyalty and deprive you of love and strength, you who see your very existence threatened by circumstances you cannot control so that you hardly know how to hold the tattered rags of your lives together, believe me that this help is real and genuine and all these surface disturbances can serve to convince us of God's indisputable nearness and reality. Oh I know that these other things seem so much more real. But the waters of healing surge up within ourselves. God within us is like a fountain and we are guests invited to rest and refresh ourselves. We must discover this fountain within ourselves and let its healing waters flow over the parched land of our lives. Then the desert will blossom. He wants to quicken you. The word of God, given long ago, is fulfilled by his free-flowing Spirit. From within you will receive the strength and the spiritual assurance to conquer. How often I have proved this in the stress of these last dismal months of burden and depression — suddenly renewed strength would flood my whole being like sunrise. The peace after a storm that has blown itself out, the satisfaction that comes from a job well done would fill my whole being. Unless we find these inner fountains, these healing waters, no outward rest, no relaxation, will help us. But when the divine Spirit dawns on man's consciousness then he is able to surpass himself. He is filled with that peace, that holy and restoring stillness which we associate with God's presence — in a cathedral for instance, in a magnificent countryside, in a cherished friendship.

Coolness in heat

This is the second fundamental need of poor, exposed, defenceless man. He is at the mercy of inner driving forces that alternately harass and handicap him till he is almost exhausted. These compulsions come from within; the sleeping volcano bursts into life and stirs up explosive energies which send the tattered remnants of reality flying in all directions. Hot blood and violent anger, the sudden assertion of the inborn urge to tyrannise – these and many other smouldering human impulses may turn into consuming fires. Outwardly most human lives go through a period of stress and alarm; it happens as naturally as a summer thunderstorm which may break suddenly or pursue its destructive course by slow and stealthy stages piling burden on burden, trouble on trouble till the heart and shoulders of the victim are weighed down. In short man is vulnerable both to inner fire and external sparks – either can be fanned into a blaze and leave behind a path of destruction and trouble beyond human endurance. Then man is forced to look for new sources of help and restoration, for powers that can re-establish the balance and enable him to master his problems.

Coolness in heat; the Holy Spirit as the source of our power to cope with the contingencies of life. God's passion for himself which finds expression through the spirit of man, burns up a man's incipient passions. Man's individuality is thereby strengthened and intensified. He is equipped to meet the trials that assail him from both within and without; his decisions are unerring because he keeps the end in view and the measure in his hand. A courageous man is filled with the Holy Ghost; he is calm and clear headed. His chariot may indeed be drawn by spirited horses but they are well controlled.

Coolness in heat; man in the midst of life's thunderstorm. This need springs from the fact that his heart is constantly being consumed by inner fires and the wings of his spirit are forever being hindered by his own wild and irresponsible impulses. Our souls and our memories are stamped with pictures — visions of refugees, of ruined houses, shattered possessions. It has all really happened. Yet these are only pictures, the reflections of man's inborn violence, the volcanic eruptions to which he has always been prone and always will be. Human power grows impotent, human strength turns to helplessness, human spirit becomes merely an instrument whereby man may measure frightfulness and drain the cup of misery to the last dregs instead of being a weapon enabling him to cope with difficulties and conquer them. This is really a case of fire fighting fire. The Holy Spirit appeared at the beginning as tongues of fire. That is God's way of dealing with the situation. God is no destroyer of the beings he has created. His will is that all shall be forgiven and redeemed and hence his fire is not consuming but healing. And in the breath of the Spirit man grows till he can control his demoniac wildness. The holy fire of God renders man impervious to the firebrands of destruction. And at one and the same time God is both fire and water. Only those who are filled with the Holy Ghost have the courage in these times to venture a word or deed of real importance. The gift of judgment, far-sightedness, the power to undertake restoration go hand in hand with steadfastness and persistence. In times like these man must send up his cry to the Holy Ghost or he will be consumed.

Solace in woe

The third fundamental need of man. Time and time again he is reduced to weeping and wailing, both individually and collectively. Trouble usually descends upon him out of the blue, often when his spirits are highest. Often trouble breaks loose at the height of a celebration when people are at ease and thoroughly pleased with themselves, lulled by their own self-esteem. Suddenly they are forced to recognise that the high opinion they had formed of themselves was an inebriated dream and no real ecstasy. Wine-tinted dreams can fashion shapely jars from broken pots but sobriety soon shatters them. Suddenly man is faced with the naked truth and forced to make the age-old admission: I have wasted my substance. Or alternately the force of reality may come down and crush him in a very elementary fashion. All the laws he has transgressed rise in judgment on him. The triumphal march of a great life dwindles to a hard crusade, then to a procession of beggars and finally to a funeral procession that goes on and on. Once again human nature is brought up short not knowing which way to turn in this eternal circle of blood. The shriek of injured innocence mingles with the hoarse croak of despair from those who suffer chains and confinement imposed by the abuse of power and with the groans of those who perceive the universal trend and look desperately for a way out – only to discover that although they work until their hands are raw they cannot find one. All that seems to triumph is arrogance, vanity, belligerence, defamation. Such terrible waste of substance. Here we have the distress – the manifest distress – of mankind.

And again the word of comfort appears. Not a false

word that will proclaim the situation harmless but an affirmation as real as the fetters on my wrists. When the Spirit reveals itself to man it gives him certain proof of God's creative freedom, of the powerful help God is capable of extending and willing to extend. The fact that man is lifted out of himself and able to look at the situation from a new angle is in itself a great step forward. He then realises that he has resources, capacities and powers of which he previously had no notion. He can follow the undercurrents and implications better than he did before, the message and the purpose of things and circumstances become clearer. He remembers the dedicated mission of John the Baptist calling on men to repent and return to God. He is able to compare the most distressing conditions to a fertile seed; it becomes a call to sacrifice, the only thing that can restore humanity's capacity to love. Warm currents of life flood his being, breaking like streams over the wilderness and making it fruitful. I vividly recall that night in the Lehrterstrasse and how I prayed to God that he might send death to deliver me because of the helplessness and pain I felt I could no longer endure, and the violence and hatred to which I was no longer equal. How I wrestled with God that night and finally in my great need crept to him, weeping. Not until morning did a great peace come to me, a blissful awareness of light, strength and warmth, bringing with it the conviction that I *must* see this thing through and at the same time the blessed assurance that I *should* see it through. *Solace in woe*. This is the Holy Spirit, the Comforter. This is the kind of creative dialogue he conducts with mankind. These are the secret blessings he dispenses which enable a man to live and endure.

O blessed light

Again we have the word light. The light that blesses, the blissful light. These words illustrate what I was trying to say just now. Man is permitted to become conscious of God as a living reality that floods him with bliss. There are summer days when the light seems to envelop us like a tangible blessing. It can happen in a lovely alpine meadow or a rippling field of ripening grain or floating silently in a boat on a beautiful lake. Man's consciousness is intensified and he feels at one with nature and has a marvellous cognition of the ripening, healing and sanctifying powers the cosmos contains. Only a receptive, reverent and observant man can experience this. It is a faint reflection of the saint's experience of blessed light – an awareness that there are times when God enfolds his children in waves of tenderness flooding their hearts and filling their whole being with the blessed current of divine life. In God this is a constant state – the state of grace, of divine son-ship. Man is only conscious of it in rare moments of contact but such moments are sufficient to see him through long days in the wilderness and long, hopeless nights, because once he has been vouchsafed such an overwhelming experience the impression never leaves him. Thereafter he can detect God's quiet smile in all things and in all conditions and circumstances.

Fill our inmost heart

Back again to the connection between the light and the heart. Here the reference has another application. Light in this context does not primarily apply to the understanding, reason, spiritual perception. Here it represents the radiance of God's love breaking out to touch man at the very centre of his consciousness and unsealing the fountains of grace which give man a foretaste of heaven. Understanding and reason are intensified as the individual is lifted up. Under the influence of this inner illumination man becomes more clear sighted, more intuitive, wiser. He is enabled to strip the mask from falsity in circumstances and in men; he is equal to any emergency and can deal with problems more kindly than if he were in an unenlightened state – because he now knows their rightful place in the scheme of things, meets them on their own ground as it were, and sees through them to the very core of their secret hearts.

Our inmost heart really refers to the life lived intimately with God. Piety alone couldn't bring about this highly intensified radiation of the personal relationship. Friendship and love grow stronger on every plane in the loving contact of the dialogue. The same applies here. The only difference lies in the fact that here the partner is the Spirit of God for whose sanctifying presence we ardently pray.

Thy faithful

I shall have something to say later about followers of the Holy Ghost. For the moment I only want to review what I have already said and examine it more closely. Like all intimacy this relationship with the Holy Ghost rests on trusting surrender and receptivity. God's Spirit never coerces even for man's own good or to hasten his self-realisation. The dialogue thus remains a genuine dialogue even though the creative force comes only from God and seeks us out and makes contact. If ever an intimacy needed to be guarded and cherished it is this one. Any man who tries to enter this dialogue with coarse thoughts and uncouth habits will lose much grace and blessing. He will miss so many whispered words of warning, silent indications of the tender solicitude and good will of God. There are times too when God's light will break like lightning over man, descend suddenly and violently, affecting his whole existence like a great boulder torn from a hillside and crashing into a lake. And in that too there are divine pointers which an unenlightened individual may easily overlook. For a sustained continuance of the dialogue alert watchfulness and sensitive receptivity are absolutely essential. These require a more complete surrender than man in his natural state is capable of; they demand supernatural alertness, the constant crossing out of our own personal will in order that it may lose itself in God's. The trustful faith with which we approach God is the door through which the miracle of God's strength enters as he gives himself to us.

Without thy grace

An unfinished sentence, this, an incomplete theme. Therefore one shouldn't spend too much time meditating on it. Yet it has an important bearing on our life today for here we have a brief and pithy summary of all the folly and error of our race, and of its destiny. *Without thy grace.* We elected to live gracelessly, we trusted solely to our own strength, were bound only by our own laws, surrendered to our own whims and followed our own instincts. On those foundations we built our new towers. We have lifted our voices and celebrated triumphs, we have marched, we have worked, we have boasted and saved and squandered. And the outcome? Precisely *without thy grace* – a graceless life, a pitiless age, an age of inexorable fate, a time of horror and violence, of worthless life and

155

senseless death. We ought not to be surprised that such a graceless life has translated itself into the kind of manifestation we are now enduring. And we who have been dragged down into the universal collapse – which perhaps we did not try to prevent by every means in our power – must in the midst of our destiny overcome that destiny, turning it into a cry for grace and mercy, for the healing waters of the Holy Ghost. Humanity ought never again to over-rate its capabilities or delude itself as we have done. Those who survive should take these lessons to heart and preach them with inspired zeal. The graceless way of living is presumptuous and leads to disaster. Man is only truly man when he lives in unity with God.

Nothing is in man

Man is nothing without God. Sometimes we are tempted to declare that man is nothing at all. But this is because comparatively few people have the good fortune to meet a real man. After all no one is above the law of transgression – *without thy grace*. We have all taken the wrong road and our empirical experience of man has demonstrated little but weakness, incapacity and extreme helplessness. Man's yearning to excel, his desire to achieve and accomplish things indicates that his shortcomings are not fundamental but are a superficial effect. His dissatisfaction with the conditions of his earthly existence is deep seated and constantly impels him to venture to try to improve his way of life.

Man has it in him to conceive high ideals and work for their realisation but if he is honest he will recognise the fact that he can do nothing on his own. Left to himself he is incomplete, not quite a man. God is part of the definition of a man; inner unity with God is the primary

156

condition for a fulfilled and successful life. The decision to recognise this is the greatest that man can make and the only one that will rescue him from the chaos in which he is involved. About turn – back to the beginning – that is the only solution and the way to achieve life's fulfilment.

Nothing is harmless

This applies to man's make up, to his total reality. Nothing is perfect and nothing can be described as potentially harmless. In plain words this means that there is a state, a condition of reality, in which things are not only out of order but actually dangerous, poisonous, destructive. We all know, individually, that there are times when everything we attempt seems to go wrong. All our efforts turn against us and end in bitter disappointment. It also sometimes applies to whole generations, to spiritual movements, to social and economic projects and so on. We see things getting out of hand; intentions and programmes misfire, not only because the ideals have been betrayed by leaders and people, but because reality itself, proving too strong, has suddenly become antagonistic, difficult, intractable. Experience confirms the belief that facts that do not take God into account are inherently unreliable, and for sound order inherent shortcomings are fatal. There can be no progress or development when the foundations are faulty – indeed the structure then becomes definitely dangerous. In the last analysis there is no such thing as neutrality – there is absolutely nothing that does not matter. Decisions, conduct, intentions, all have either a positive or a negative value and if negative they are harmful and dangerous. Thus the sentence *nothing is harmless* should put us on our guard. The thought expressed is one in which man can recognise his need of an alliance with God, the initial and decisive step towards his own good. Anyone who rejects this partnership lays up a store of trouble for himself and is definitely acting against his own interests.

But our prayer applies to the terms of personal intimacy on which we ought to live with the Spirit of God, the Holy Ghost. And here the same thing is true, even more true. Intimacy with the Holy Ghost is grace in concrete form and is therefore a contact, a partnership. Moreover by his own being the Holy Ghost strengthens our spirit and gives it the capacity to achieve a fulfilled and successful life. He gives us mastery over our inherent weaknesses, our liability to err, our inhibitions and handicaps so that we not only conquer them but can rise above them. Man in a state of grace, through the Holy Ghost, is more capable of conducting his own life successfully and is also better equipped to help others. In his handling of everyday affairs he has clearer insight and better judgment, he is kinder and more generous. He bestows blessings and receives them.

Wash what is stained

Toil, heat and grief express fundamental conditions of human nature which always make themselves felt as long as man is on his journey through life. They are not always so abnormally prevalent as they are today but they are nevertheless an indispensable part of man's existence. And only when he fails to go through life in partnership with God do these things get the upper hand bursting all bounds and overwhelming man with trouble of all kinds.

I am not concerned here with the material needs of man but with his own degeneration, his blunted faculties and spiritual poverty – all the burdens in fact which the kind of existence he leads have introduced into his life and which have now become characteristic of his nature. Just as there are virtues that can be acquired so also there are faults that result from repetition such as habitual unawareness of individuality, perpetual relinquishment of powers of decision, permanent weakening of the sense of reality, and so on. Faced with these shortcomings man finds himself under a terrible strain and utterly helpless. If he loses his material possessions his vision is clear enough to enable him to regain them. He might through carelessness or sheer foolishness or some ill judged idea allow his right hand to be cut off or suffer some other form of mutilation and then he has no personal power to put the thing right. These are misfortunes a man might suffer but they do not come from any limitations of human nature but from the wrong use of freedom — hence man must accept responsibility for the mis-use of his free will. Being prone to such errors of judgment the only thing he can do is to turn again and again to God praying earnestly that the Holy Ghost may take pity on his failings and let the healing current flow freely through his life.

With an honesty that is quite shattering the verses that follow list man's most urgent requirements. Again and again they bring up the dominant failings of human life. And we must admit that all men experience both these failings and the needs mentioned earlier. And we today, perhaps more than at any other time, have fallen back on our last reserves as human beings and made serious inroads on them. For us the borderline is more sharply defined and our failure more obvious and more keenly felt. It all stresses the fact that it is more than time contemporary western man returned to his natural human status determined by his relationship with God in humility, contact and unity. Of course we must clearly understand that God does not exist merely as a sort of medicine for ailing humanity. In the first place the Lord says: I will renew you, and in the second place it is not that God exists for man and his well-being, but that the man who does not exist for God and live up to all the conditions God has laid down or may lay down, is his own enemy and murderer.

There are moments in every man's life when he is filled with self disgust, when consciousness of failure tears the mask from self assurance and self justification and reality stands revealed — even if only for a moment. Occasionally such a moment produces a permanent change and the mask is not resumed. Man's natural tendency is to avoid these moments of truth. Pride, cowardice, and above all an intuitive feeling that the only way out of the situation will be to humble oneself and submit, tempt a man to declare reality unreal and to pronounce the counterfeit genuine.

The shock may come when a great wrong, or a succession of mischances, has sapped man's self confidence and forced him to take a closer look at himself. Everything depends on whether he takes this seriously or passes it off as a moment of 'weakness' from which he speedily 'recovers'. In that case his last state is worse than his first — he becomes immunised to error, no longer able to distinguish the false from the true. Then we get clichés like 'self determination', the 'right to live', 'hunger for life' and so on. When this happens in the case of a gifted person he can easily become an evil influence leading others astray, scattering sparks that ignite the inflammable material and bring about historic catastrophes. Such individuals are capable of dragging whole generations to ruin. Their contemporaries suddenly find themselves in a vicious circle, sharing responsibility for evils they are unable to rectify.

On the other hand by divine grace a man may be suddenly raised to a consciousness of how near he is to God. Then, too, he is bound to be shocked by the truth of his own unworthiness. None of us can escape the admission that we have made sad mistakes and to some extent bungled our lives. By acknowledging his fault man recognises his weakness and his dependence on divine help and recognises also the danger of concluding an easy peace with the weaknesses of his own nature. Coming to terms with things our conscience cannot approve means that we must share the responsibility for them because they have our assent.

There is only one way to salvation and it is not achieved by trying to escape or failing to acknowledge our fault. We are saved not by denying our failures but by looking at them honestly and acknowledging them. This need not distress us – it is a salutary experience to be roused now and then to recognition of our mistakes and to make a fresh start. Woe to the man who gets bogged down in error, resigning himself to it through sheer fatigue – when that happens everything is lost. If in the midst of sin man can hold on to the finer impulses of his nature they will show him the way back to his true self. Sin always sullies and sometimes distorts reality. Only the Lord of creation is capable of restoring it and he is always willing to do so. All the sinner has to do is submit to God's word and surrender himself to the healing will. Submission is his contribution to the cure. But the healing, creative, intervention of God cannot be dispensed with and this is most potent at the moment of contact with the Holy Ghost. It

161

is in the bliss of that contact that man comes to full awareness of his human limitations and the unworthiness of sin. And again all that he can do is to surrender himself absolutely in order that the Spirit of God may do its work in the unity of contact.

The Holy Ghost floods our being like a healing stream and no blemish can withstand its cleansing power. *Wash what is stained.* This must be the prayer of all who long for unity with God in the core of their being. Great benevolence and grace are called for and God does not withhold these from his creation. Man cannot live without this creative contact with his Maker and these fountains are unsealed by honest and complete surrender. This is the indispensable act on man's part — surrender and prayer.

Water what is barren

We have to keep reminding ourselves of the underlying theme of the Whitsuntide liturgy — the devout dialogue between the worshipper and the creative Spirit. When song dies in the heart and the inner fountains have dried up the waste land of our life becomes a barren wilderness swept by raging sand storms. There are moments of exaltation and inspiration when the world seems almost too small and the stars are very near — but this is often a kind of creative drunkenness quickly dispelled on sober awakening to the realities of human weakness. Some men have a natural creative gift, more penetrating insight and a more skilful hand than others for the shaping of intractable material — but there are limits to this too; genius is also subject to frustration and sudden disappointment.

There are two kinds of sterility — personal barrenness and the barrenness of whole generations. A man may be sterile not only in his personal life but also, and much more terribly, in his contact with God, in the living dialogue with his Creator.

And a generation can be sterile; suddenly the creative fruitfulness of a whole race may dry up. Creative ideas are no longer born, nothing of any note is produced in art, literature, politics, philosophy, theology or religion.

These manifestations require much thought. They cannot merely be noted as facts and left at that. They are conditioned by fundamental laws of our existence.

The obvious and easiest explanation, which traces back the failure of creative substance to exhaustion and fatigue, simply does not suffice. There is not only supra-normal impulse and fertility — there is also a sub-normal level of sterility. And the fact of creative productivity ceasing indicates that fundamental laws are involved and that fundamental health is affected. And if this is conceded we must recognise that we are not concerned only with great creative achievements, though these also come under the same laws since the pre-requisites for great achievement are exemplified by man in his relationship with his fellow creatures and with God. When man gets to a stage where adoration is no longer fruitful or seems strange and contrary to his nature, when his love has degenerated into superficial emotion and he doesn't want anything else, when he really only exists as a caricature of himself, then the sources dry up and man's own wilderness starts to spread and encroach on the green and fertile land. The immediate cause may lie in outward conditions that sap man's strength or regiment him into narrow channels. But underneath it all there is still the fundamental fact that man himself has lost his sense of values, the instinct that should enable him to judge rightly. Another factor

163

may be the false image he has formed of his own potentialities, either through conceit or through collective wrong thinking. In any case the actual cause is the failure of his critical judgment and his obstinate determination to go his own way, following his own blind impulses.

Here too the only solution is to re-establish the partnership with God. This is the only order by which a man can properly regulate his life. It is the pattern to which he was created and the one he has got to live by. Where objective circumstances consequent on wrong decisions have become so hard and intolerable that they bow man down it is no use waiting for a new order to emerge from a change of heart. Active steps must be taken to reorganise life in accordance with God's law, even at the expense, if need be, of a real clash.

This cannot be done without God's help. May he stir men's hearts and give the necessary vision and courage to make the decisive step.

In the last analysis it is our lack of vitality that causes fatigue and exhaustion. The burdens God lays on us can be heavy and the road dreary and exhausting. Man can only make an effort and bear strain up to a certain point. There are limits to his endurance and beyond that point he needs help from outside.

And there is another wilderness which he must cross — the wilderness God ordains both as a test and a means of redemption. Let him go towards it bravely — but not without earnestly and trustfully reaching out for God's guiding hand. These wildernesses must be mastered — that of loneliness, of fear, of depression, of sacrifice. God who created wildernesses also made the streams that bring forth fruitfulness when they flow over barren land. Prayer and trust in his goodness bring his promises to pass.

Heal what is wounded

Man is in great distress when he is wounded. The desire to be whole and fulfilled is so strong that he regards every wound as an injustice. The further he is from fulfilment the greater the heights he will have to scale in his endeavour to attain it and as he goes on he realises that no progress can be made without getting wounded now and then. Even when he is in sober earnest and honestly adheres to the partnership he still has to fight his way through to the hard core of reality, and suffer sorrow, privation and pain in his own person. Dumb nature hits out at a man through its very dumbness and the rigidity of its rhythmic constitution which does not yield to man's will without a struggle – and especially to that ultimate will which represents his innermost self. Man attacks man in enmity, deliberately and thoughtlessly, through greed, through indifference, through hatred and sometimes through love. There is no end to the wounds men can inflict on each other, and sometimes the hardest blows of all are those sustained when God himself seems to be inflicting pain on his poor creatures. He named those who mourn and those who suffer among the blessed but so often that blessing seems to be nothing more than a promise, while man chafes under the conviction that his current suffering is due to an act of God. Poor wretch – he some times feels he would like to crawl into a hole like some stricken animal and hide where no more harm can come to him. But even that is no use. The ties of love, of duty, the bonds of everyday existence keep us at our posts in our greatest distress. And many have to carry not only their own misery around with them but to share the need and the sickness of others, of the great mass of humanity grown silent and weary.

I have frequently referred in these meditations to the dangers and setbacks man encounters at every level of existence, and I don't want to go into that again. Let us leave the solution of these problems to prayer. It is best that all the suffering and misery should be gathered up in one great cry for help. There are times when this is the only thing that can be done. When all else fails we remember God and appeal for help. And in the stillness of this holy contact help assuredly comes. Sooner or later our fruitless efforts to escape from our entanglements must cease; we must realise their futility. Straining against the pricks never helps — it only produces more worries. We must grow quiet enough to realise God's omnipresence, to feel his comforting hand and open our hearts from within, silently, letting his healing will have its way. Then the waters will flow over the arid soil and things will start to grow again. If only we keep still. God permits many wounds — but there are also miracles. We are today — individually and collectively — fainting from want and loss of blood. Things have gone so far that no one can help us any more — neither friend, nor goodwill, nor comfort can do us any good. Our last resource is to turn to the creative Spirit, the Holy Ghost, which is ready and willing to pour out on us the healing power of our Father, God.

Because of this man should never despair even in his darkest hours. He should remember that God shares his life, that through the Holy Ghost he can be on the most intimate terms with God and that God is always there, when outward pressure is at its worst, helping him to carry his burdens over the roughest places on his weary road. There is no fibre of his being that the healing Spirit cannot reach as long as he is willing to let it do its creative, healing work. It goes on in silence within him and he should remind himself constantly that in alliance with God he possesses powers of recuperation which enable him to endure the most grievous wounds without flinching and go on meeting the demands life makes on him. He should have this inner confidence, not mere self reliance, but because he knows beyond a shadow of doubt that God is sharing his life with him.

The worst wounds that can be inflicted on man, or that he can inflict on himself, are those of evil. When faith wavers, hope disappears, love grows cold, adoration ceases, doubt nags and the whole life is shrouded like a winter landscape in snow, when hatred and arrogance predominate, life is mortally wounded. That is the time to get into reverse, and let the Holy Ghost work from within building up a new life. From God's view point the world looks quite different and we must at all costs get back to the divine point of view. And a great many situations must be subjected to this process of conversion. The man who insists on isolation and never grows conscious of the inner presence of the Spirit is doomed to failure after failure. I am proving this each day and each hour. If I had tried to cope with all this mountain of trouble unaided I should have reached the end of my tether long ago. Natural logic keeps forcing its evil conclusions, like poison, on one's consciousness. To counter them one has to apply the logic of healing, of guidance and submission, on which decisions can be based when they have been patiently arrived at through prayer. The Holy Ghost constantly helps me over my hurdles in the small hours. I am aware of this and I do not doubt it. I could never have accomplished any of this on my own. Not even that night in the Lehrterstrasse. God heals. The healing strength of God lives in me and with me.

Bend what is rigid

Life knows nothing more injurious than creeping paralysis. A paralysed life is utterly impoverished whether it realises its condition or whether it has become so accustomed to paralysis that it thinks it normal. Movement, animation, is a primary law of life. It goes hand in hand with unfolding, growth. Sensation which is inherent in all living things, craves for change; inertia is foreign to it because the very vitality of living drives it on to the desired goal of fulfilment. Paralysis is the exact opposite. It brings existence to a standstill at one particular point; it cuts across the law of progress with an untimely desire for a fixed destination.

Man can be rigid in many ways. He can have a one-track mind like the rich young man in the gospel. God would be doing such a man a kindness in destroying his possessions before calling him to the last judgment. This paralysis in the realm of things, this fixation about property, riches, gold, jewels, art and good living was characteristic of the last century. One half of the world's population lost their souls to material possessions; the other half spent their time protesting, not at the danger to mankind through this kind of bondage, but at the fact that it was not possible for them to lose their souls in the same way because they had not yet succeeded in gaining such possessions. Recent wars have destroyed houses, goods and much more besides. If a new freedom and a new outlook do not emerge from this destruction mankind will once again have missed a great opportunity.

Even more dangerous is that inner paralysis which induces man to betray the fundamental laws of his existence. No longer 'living to all truth, to all goodness' he pulls up short, sets himself apart, rests on his laurels and leads the life of a pensioner. He no longer strains with all his might to achieve ideals, reaching for the stars. The command to love God with all his heart, with all his mind and with all his strength no longer has any meaning for him; he treats it as something handed down like a legend, something that has served its turn and can be thrown aside. All the truths have already been discovered, he thinks – no need to go to the trouble of looking for any more. The world has grown dumb – he no longer hears the underground rumblings as the secret forces collect their strength for the great fulfilment which can only be brought about by man's conscious recognition and decision. Destiny, and God's Spirit operating from within, can save this kind of man from the hard fate in store by re-kindling the divine spark in his heart. Here is a case that emphatically calls for bending, loosening, melting, making the intractable pliable. Present day man's incapacity for love, for reverence, for appreciation has its roots in arrogance and in this petrifying of existence.

A pliable nature is a gift of grace rather than the outcome of effort or the operation of fate. In all sincerity man must loyally observe the rule of the road along which he is travelling. Then the dialogue will be maintained and he will remain a genuine partner in divine freedom and vitality.

Fate may be the cause of a paralysis which is the grimmest of all. When life itself transfixes a man, tying him hand and foot, shutting him up in a prison with no possible outlet, of what use then are all decisions to live abundantly? The paralysis of fear, the hardening brought about by bitter experience are often a mere defensive armour, but they can also endanger life itself. Only when God's strength plays a part in the drama will the inner vitality hold out, even if man falls. The restorative power of the Spirit must refresh man's nature from within rendering him capable of resisting temptation and of holding his own, no matter what fate may have in store for him. The love of God, and the patient loving hands of those whose lives have not been afflicted with paralysis, will help him in his struggle.

A life that has hardened into numbness is mortally sick. All that is vital in life succumbs to the hardening process. A numbed man deludes himself into believing that he cannot hear the inner voice that calls on him to shake off this numbness and rise out of himself. He is bound and fettered to himself and wastes away in that condition. He becomes incapable of living faith, as he is incapable of entering into the dialogue, the fundamental form of creative life in every respect. True faith, reverence, respect, love, adoration – all these are forms of the dialogue and all of them are stifled in the numbness brought about by the hardening of heart. So a man really ought to make every effort to maintain the dialogue and not to miss a single moment of contact with the invisible partner. More grievous than any external hardness or difficulty is this inner numbness, whether it results from habit, or fear, or shock, from pettiness or pride.

In the creative dialogue man finds himself and makes closer acquaintance with his underlying motives and his background. Hence the prayer for bending is actually a plea for his own life. Oh how a life can suffer from its own hardening and numbness. When I think back I realise how conceited I was about my own firmness. It was all self-deception and arrogance, this fine idea I had of my independence and so on. I had my suspicions about it even then, for I found that whenever I caused anyone pain that pain hurt me also. Contact with God helped me at such times and I noticed that the more honest it became the more I was forced to give up my arrogant attitude and my unloving approach. But I really owe the quickening of my intercourse with God chiefly to the intensifying of intercourse with my fellow-man, which broke much fresh ground in me and brought it under cultivation for the first time.

When a man's heart softens and loses its numbness he actually brings about his own liberation. Like all surrender that is not prompted by creative assent this can be a painful business. But it is restorative and a step towards freedom – the torrent at last finds an outlet to its own ocean. The overcoming of icy isolation, of lack of love and self-sufficiency – that is the task of the Holy Ghost in man.

Melt what is frozen

In a collect – I think it is that of the day dedicated to St Francis's stigmata – the words 'world grown cold' occur. As the world turned to ice it was the time and the hour of this saint of love. *A world grown cold:* love turned cold is the deadly fate that threatens all life and must be overcome at all costs. Man should recognise clearly what this horror means, whence it comes and how devastating it can be.

Science maintains that our earth will eventually end in another ice age. That is as may be; at the present stage of knowledge it may be regarded as possible. No one can tell what the future may hold in the way of new impulses and changes of emphasis as developments proceed. But no one can dispute that the culture of the west, where documents and monuments are at present being rapidly destroyed, has frozen to death. Man is only a man, and great, in so far as he is capable of loving. In the west it is long since men loved greatly and had a passion for the absolute. They have had passions for things, for power, for authority, for pleasure, for possessions, but they have not been capable of a genuine passion for mankind. Everything had to have a purpose or an object. Man was no longer the target but only the means through which others could heighten and multiply their own experiences. Our hearts no longer trembled when we thought of ultimate realities like God, man, mission, and so on. Things were proclaimed, passed on and practised as before but the actual creative source within us, the genuine impulse, the great surrender, even the passion, was lacking.

It is not easy to revive a smouldering fire. When man has strayed from the current of reality he can do nothing about it at any rate on his own. At best he can revive his memory, give the assent of his will and pray for the fire from heaven that prepares, transforms and rekindles.

The Holy Ghost is God's passion for himself. Man must make contact with this passion, must play his part in completing the circuit. Then true love will reign again in the world and man will be capable of living to the full. The indwelling presence of God must take possession of our senses, draw us out of ourselves, in order that we may be capable of genuine assent and contact. God must ratify himself in us and through us; then we shall live as we should. Then the holy fire will again become the heart of the earth and remain so.

Bend what is rigid – melt what is frozen

Two characteristic features of our age come up before the seat of judgment – middle class respectability and the bureaucratic Church.

At one time the middle class style of life had its virtues and served a purpose. It was always threatened and it was also always a potential danger because it allied itself with human weakness and ran the risk that the possessions man hoarded, and which he needed for his task and mission, would end by mastering him. This was his particular form of numbness and hardening; the sense of duty died out and what remained was middle class gluttony, idleness, comfort, ease and all that went with material possessions. Dividends, stock, shares, bank balances – these were the symbols of respectability, the ideals men strived for. There arose a type of man to whose hearts one might almost say God himself could find no access, because they were so hedged around with security and insurance. The type still flourishes. It laid down the lines on which our present progress is developing. The type has not been overcome because all the counter-movements have failed to negative the type – they merely object to the exclusion of sections of humanity from the type. Most modern movements set off with the object of enabling their adherents to live in the best possible material style. And even where the times and the spiritual connections have here and there carried the movements on they have still clung to the old middle class mould in middle class imperialism.

It is a pity that so much that gave momentum to the

old system must now be brought up for judgment before *bend* and *melt* which alone can rouse mankind from its lethargy. And that there are so many men the heat of the fire has not yet reached. A new alert type of man must be born of this trial of fire and of the penetrative radiance of the Spirit. He must be awake and alive, this new man, fully responsible, with far seeing eyes and a listening heart. His soul must respond to the marching song and his spirit must carry the standard of freedom he has found and to which he has sworn allegiance.

The other type which must appear for judgment is no less important and quite as numerous in present day life. In fact men of this type inside the Church are largely responsible for its bureaucratic pattern. The Church has made its own contribution to the emergence of the middle class. And the middle class has lost no opportunity to take advantage of the Church and to establish the ideals of human weakness, riches, power, luxury and security in the Church.

Of course there must be administration in the Church — statistics, auditors, official seals and so on. Nothing can alter that. But while it is in the nature of things that such organisation should be centralised, in the ecclesiastical sphere this should be as little noticeable as possible. Man as man has become subjectively and objectively submerged, impersonalised, under ecclesiastical life and ecclesiastical guidance. It is useless to quote a list of examples. Only one thing need be stressed. The rule that ordains that leaders should have neither names nor faces has encouraged regimentation in our lives quite as much as the anonymous act and the control of the State, economics and political parties.

Here, too, appeals to a vital, personally courageous

existence will be in vain until God calls the Church and its present system to account before the judgment seat of *bend* and *melt*. 'None can pass through fire without being transformed.' When we have passed through a hundred doors and all our bridges are burnt we get some inkling of the immense distance that must be covered if the name of God is to pass our lips. The Spirit, the life-giver, will help us emerge from all this rubble, not as human ruins but as men with new horizons and new courage. We must forget a great deal and forsake much and we must invest a great deal more if we are to win back the whole. The earth is being ploughed and new seed sown. Let us cherish God's freedom and surrender ourselves to the truth and vitality of the Spirit.

Correct what is wrong

One of the saddest and most significant things about modern life is that it lacks instinct. Loss of instinct is the greatest deprivation either for a tamed animal or a human being who is exhausted. Men today are completely without instinct. Under the fatal burden of our civilisation, the overwhelming weight of our titanic dreams, the futile waste of our so-called self realisation and other vague ideas we have lost our natural instinct. And the mechanisation and reorganisation of our religious life has taken away our supernatural instinct as well. Very seldom is a natural taste for religion (which is a characteristic of the man who consciously yields himself to the indwelling Spirit) met with nowadays. The certainty which enabled us to distinguish between good and evil by our own inner standard, to decide between useful and harmful, between wisdom and folly, has vanished. This explains the immature behaviour of so many Christians today. It has a much deeper cause than faulty upbringing or inadequate instruction. The religious profession, like other professions, suffers from this same lack.

Our deviation from the right road underlines the fundamental errors and the need for immediate repentance. As the whole theme of this prayer is life in the intimacy of the Holy Ghost, the loving creative contact between the Spirit of life and man the created being, I think it is especially pertinent to the correction of this lack of instinct. Both as individual Christians, and as the corporate community, the Church, we have in recent times failed in our dealings with our fellow man, failed in our assessment of situations and spiritual realities, in the art of leading men, in the presentation of our doctrine and in much else besides. We have every reason to be shocked and ashamed. Of course the Church still has skilful apologists, clever and compelling preachers, wise leaders; but the simple confidence that senses the right course and proceeds to act on it almost unconsciously is just not there.

Among the gifts of the Holy Ghost are listed prudence, wisdom and piety. These are natural attributes which provide penetration, the power to see connecting links to divine underlying factors and basic causes. These are the 'intuitive' faculties with which the Holy Ghost endows us and which he keeps alive in us by his own life. They give us the 'single eye' and safeguard us against blind conflict with reality which must in the end do us harm.

Give to thy faithful

Faith is the point of contact. I have already pointed out that this wonderful life of spirit can only grow and unfold in the sphere and atmosphere of personal intimacy. The first step is faith and that means faith as personal surrender. There is far more to this than the bare acceptance of truth as the rock on which God's Church is built. This is the very least a man can offer in the way of assent and receptivity. Anyone determined to limit his acceptance to the things he can grasp and understand is not going to get very close to the living God. Faith is man's first step away from himself and towards God as centre and absolute reality, to the exclusion of self and all pseudo realities. And the decision has to be translated into one personal thing – unconditional loyalty. Only then does it become vital, alive: in that moment our real consciousness of the Holy Ghost is born. But it only becomes active in us when we can realise it as the personal will of God for us and give the corresponding personal answer. Life has the same fundamental pattern even in the realm of the supernatural – the personal dialogue is the basis of spiritual vitality. Give to *thy* faithful the prayer says. It is exactly like the intercourse of two healthy human beings – the heart dares to mate with another because it finds itself at home with the chosen comrade whose worth is recognised. The Spirit does not use force, breaking in like a thief. God's holy will never coerces but responds to the cry of willing assent. And when that cry is raised the slightest movement of the heart is sufficient to stir the ocean of God's munificent love into full flood.

We must make veneration of the Holy Ghost and the plea for his coming and his blessing our heart's constant prayer, particularly today as we see more and more what the destruction going on round us really means. It is in conditions like these that the word takes on its full meaning for us. Only in prayer can we go on, can we rise to the heights and use our full capacity for life.

Who trust in thee

Confidence is the fruit of faith. It is the condition that has not yet attained the full blessing of love but it embodies the sense of security we experience when we have firm ground under our feet, a foundation we can rely on. It puts man's doubts to rest and allows him a sense of peace because he knows he can depend on the integrity he has built up and on his capacity to measure up to life's demands and bear whatever burdens are in store. The decision I spoke of just now in relation to personal faith becomes something final, irrevocable and is the basis for the ensuing decision. Confidence means that something can be relied on in face of all doubt and reservation and appearances to the contrary.

But the condition of personal trust and confidence is something more. We can trust in things of proven value or those vouched for by reliable people. But this is because we have confidence in ourselves, in our expert knowledge and judgment or in the trustworthiness of the guarantors. But where the relationship between two persons is concerned, trust is only possible as a personal intimacy – not necessarily the supreme intimacy of love although love is the ultimate blessing and the harvest of trust.

The relationship between man and God, in spite of the distance between them and the humble reverence necessary on man's part, is a relationship built on personal trust. God bases many of his promises on the trust man should place in him. Many miracles and graces depend on the trust with which they are prayed for and expected. In this respect man has a certain advantage over God – an advantage he rarely realises and so often fails to make use of. Our Lord called his disciples men of little faith when they did not trust him to cope with a few manifestations, laws of nature or consequences of natural logic. We must at the very least arrive at a state of mind that will make certain things do not fail because we had insufficient faith to let God handle them.

Realisation of our wonderful life in the Holy Ghost also rests on our trust. Despite our indwelling Spirit we often feel tired and frightened and dis-heartened because we do not trust the Spirit of God sufficiently for him to be able to make something of us. We believe more in our own unworthiness than in the creative impulse of God – who is living our lives jointly with us. It all hinges on trust, on whether we are willing to receive God's creative blessing and let it fulfil our lives making us efficient, living souls. Blessed are those that hunger and thirst . . .

THE LAST STAGE

I AFTER THE VERDICT

It has become an odd sort of life I am leading. It is so easy to get used to existence again that one has to keep reminding oneself that death is round the corner. Condemned to death. The thought refuses to penetrate; it almost needs force to drive it home. The thing that makes this kind of death so singular is that one feels so vibrantly alive with the will to live unbroken and every nerve tingling with life. A malevolent external force is the only thing that can end it. The usual intimations of approaching death are therefore lacking. One of these days the door will open, the gaoler will say 'Pack up. The car will be here in half an hour.' We have often heard this and know exactly what it is like.

Actually I had thought to be taken to Plotzensee straight away last Thursday evening. But a new timetable is in force and we, apparently, are the first people to come under it. Or could it be that appeals have been made? I hardly think so. Here everything is subjective – not even bureaucratic procedure but undisguised subjectivity. The man Freisler is able, nervous, vain and arrogant. He is playing a part and his opponent must be made to look inferior. In this sort of dialogue the advantage of having the upper hand is obvious.

While it was all going on I felt as if I were a mere spectator. It was rather like a bad Pullach debate only that the defence kept changing and the accuser decided who was in the right. His fellow judges, the 'people', were a bunch of ordinary, dutiful individuals who had put on their Sunday suits very ceremoniously for the occasion and took themselves very seriously indeed sitting there in judgment with Herr President in his red robe. They were good biddable SS men, obediently fulfilling the role of the 'people' – which is to say 'yes'.

Everything was as per schedule – nothing missing; the Grand Entrance with an awe-inspiring muster of police – each of us had two men with him. Behind us, the public, mostly gestapo and so on; their faces are good-natured, average faces, very accustomed to this sort of thing, the average type representing 'the' Germany. The other Germany is not represented, or is in the process of being condemned to death. All the performance needed was an overture and a finale at the end – or at least a fanfare.

The proceedings themselves were handled slickly and ruthlessly – so ruthlessly that no word in the defendants' favour was even permitted. The only questions asked were those that suited the accusers' purpose and the findings, naturally, were in accordance.

Our case was aimed at the destruction of Moltke and myself and all the rest was mere window dressing. I knew from the moment we began that my fate was already sealed. The questions were all prepared and followed a definite plan and woe betide any answer that did not fit into the pre-arranged pattern. Scholasticism and Jesuitism were paraded as the real villains. It is a common belief that a Jesuit commits a crime every time he draws breath. He can say and do and prove whatever he likes – no one ever believes him.

The slanders on the Church, incidents singled out from Church history, the smirching of the Order and so on were very grim. I had to keep a tight grip on myself to stop myself exploding. But if I had let go it would have ruined all our chances. It was a great opportunity for the actor to declare his opponent a clever, dangerous, beaten man and then show off as being, himself, immensely superior. From the moment he started it was all over. I strongly advise my brothers in the Order to keep away from these trials where one is not a human being but an object. And all under an inflated rigmarole of legal terms and phrases. Just before this I had been reading Plato who said that the greatest injustice is that performed in the name of justice.

Our own crime was that of heresy against the third Reich. Someone ought to remind Freisler what would have happened if Moltke's defence plan had been used. And how many of the men he (F) has condemned are being missed now. Anyone who dares cast any doubts on the Nazi system is of course a heretic – and former judgments on heretics are child's play compared to the refined and deadly retribution practised by these people.

Moltke's plight might not have been so bad if he had not been 'tied up with the Church' which laid him open to the charge of 're-christianising intentions'. He had consorted with bishops and Jesuits. What fools we were when we tried to make preparation for this trial – it had nothing whatever to do with facts or truth. This was not a court of justice but a function. An unmistakable echo and nothing else. I just can't understand how any man can go on doing this sort of thing day after day.

The final session was on Thursday and all round everything else went on as usual – rather like a prize-giving in a small school which hadn't even the proper room for it. I thought Moltke and I would be taken to the Plotzensee immediately afterwards but we are still here.

185

The sentence seemed just as unreal as the proceedings of the two previous days. I kept the Host with me and before the final session I said Mass and took communion – my last meal. I wanted to be prepared. But here I am, still waiting.

Up to now the Lord has helped me wonderfully. I am not yet scared and not yet beaten. The hour of human weakness will no doubt come and sometimes I am depressed when I think of all the things I hoped to do. But I am now a man internally free and far more genuine and realised than I was before. Only now have I sufficient insight to see the thing as a whole.

To be quite honest I do not yet believe in my execution. I don't know why. Perhaps our Father, God, has some great grace in store for me and will enable me to pass through this wilderness without having to perish in it. During the proceedings, even when it was clear there would be no miracle, I felt lifted above it all and quite untouched by all that was going on. Was that a miracle? If not, what was it? I am really in some embarrassment before God and must think it out.

All these long months of misfortune fit into some special pattern. From the first I was so sure everything would turn out well. God always strengthened me in that conviction. These last few days I have doubted and wondered whether my will to live has been sublimated into religious delusions or something like that. Yet all these unmistakable moments of exaltation in the midst of misery; my confidence and unshakable faith even when I was being beaten up, the certain 'in spite of it all' that kept my spirits up and made me so sure that they would not succeed in destroying me; those consolations in prayer and in the Blessed Sacrament, the moments of grace; the signs I prayed for that were vouchsafed again and again – must I put them all away from me now? Does God ask the sacrifice which I will not deny him – or is he testing my faith and my trust to the last limit of endurance? As I was being taken to Berlin for the preliminary hearing I suddenly remembered the unexploded bomb in St Ignatius's House and quite distinctly I heard the words 'It will not explode'.

And the second special thing about this week is that everything I did to better my situation went wrong and in fact made it worse. It was the same during the recent hearing. The change of lawyers which at first seemed so promising was a bad mistake. As the new man became aware of the anti-Jesuit complex he told me, while the proceedings were still in progress, that as a matter of fact he was against Jesuits too. Sending Freisler the pamphlet *Man and History* was a mistake also – it only gave him the impression I was clever and therefore more dangerous. Statistics prepared for our defence were used against us. The whole proceedings led to one disaster after another. And on top of all this the quite unforeseen misfortune that we remain here, still alive, when we had prepared ourselves to die last Thursday. And so on.

What is God's purpose in all this? Is it a further lesson with regard to complete freedom and absolute surrender? Does he want us to drain the chalice to the dregs and are these hours of waiting preparation for an extraordinary Advent? Or is he testing our faith?

What should I do to remain loyal – go on hoping despite the hopelessness of it all? Or should I relax? Ought I to resign myself to the inevitable and is it cowardice not to do this and to go on hoping? Should I simply stand still, free and ready to take whatever God sends? I can't yet see the way clear before me; I must go on praying for light and guidance. And then there is the accepted sacrifice of the past seven months. It is terrible the way a man keeps on going over these things in his heart. But at least I will look at them honestly under the impulse of the Holy Spirit.

When I compare my icy calm during the court proceedings with the fear I felt, for instance, during the bombing of Munich, I realise how much I have changed. But the question keeps coming back – was this change the purpose of it all – or is this inner exaltation and help the miracle I asked for?

I don't know. Logically there is no hope at all. The atmosphere here, so far as I am concerned, is so hostile that an appeal has not the slightest chance of succeeding. So is it madness to hope – or conceit, or cowardice, or grace? Often I just sit before God looking at him questioningly.

But one thing is gradually becoming clear – I must surrender myself completely. This is seed-time, not harvest. God sows the seed and some time or other he will do the reaping. The one thing I must do is to make sure the seed falls on fertile ground. And I must arm myself against the pain and depression that sometimes almost defeat me. If this is the way God has chosen – and everything indicates that it is – then I must willingly and without rancour make it my way. May others at some future time find it possible to have a better and happier life because we died in this hour of trial.

I ask my friends not to mourn, but to pray for me and help me as long as I have need of help. And to be quite clear in their own minds that I was sacrificed, not conquered. It never occurred to me that my life would end like this. I had spread my sails to the wind and set my course for a great voyage, flags flying, ready to brave every storm that blew. But it could be they were false flags or my course wrongly set or the ship a pirate and its cargo contraband. I don't know. And I will not sink to cheap jibes at the world in order to raise my spirits. To be quite honest I don't want to die, particularly now that I feel I could do more important work and deliver a new message about values I have only just discovered and understood. But it has turned out otherwise. God keep me in his providence and give me strength to meet what is before me.

It only remains for me to thank a great many people for their help and loyalty and belief in me, and for the love they have shown me. First and foremost my brethren in the Order who gave me a genuine and beautiful vision of life. And the many sincere people I was privileged to meet. I remember very clearly the times when we were able to meet freely and discuss the tasks in front of us. Do not give up, ever. Never cease to cherish the people in your hearts – the poor forsaken and betrayed people who are so helpless. For in spite of all their outward display and loud self assurance, deep down they are lonely and frightened. If through one man's life there is a little more love and kindness, a little more light and truth in the world, then he will not have lived in vain.

Nor must I forget those to whom I owe so much. May those I have hurt forgive me – I am sorry for having injured them. May those to whom I have been untrue forgive me – I am sorry for having failed them. May those to whom I have been proud and overbearing forgive me – I repent my arrogance. And may those to whom I have been unloving forgive me – I repent my hardness.

Oh yes – long hours spent in this cell with fettered wrists and my body and spirit tormented must have broken down a great deal that was hard in me. Much that was unworthy and worthless has been committed to the flames.

So farewell. My offence is that I believed in Germany and her eventual emergence from this dark hour of error and distress, that I refused to accept that accumulation of arrogance, pride and force that is the Nazi way of life, and that I did this as a Christian and a Jesuit. These are the values for which I am here now on the brink waiting for the thrust that will send me over. Germany will be reborn, once this time has passed, in a new form based on reality with Christ and his Church recognised again as being the answer to the secret yearning of this earth and its people, with the Order the home of proved men – men who today are hated because they are misunderstood in their voluntary dedication or feared as a reproach in the prevailing state of pathetic, immeasurable human bondage. These are the thoughts with which I go to my death.

And so to conclude I will do what I so often did with my fettered hands and what I will gladly do again and again as long as I have a breath left – I will give my blessing. I will bless this land and the people; I will bless the Church and pray that her fountains may flow again fresher and more freely; I will bless all those who have believed in me and trusted me, all those I have wronged and all those who have been good to me – often too good.

God be with you and protect you. Help my poor old parents through these days of trial and keep them in your thoughts. God help you all.

I will honestly and patiently await God's will. I will

trust him till they come to fetch me. I will do my best to ensure that this blessing, too, shall not find me broken and in despair.

11 LETTER TO THE BRETHREN

Dear Brethren,

Here I am at the parting of the ways and I must take the other road after all. The death sentence has been passed and the atmosphere is so charged with enmity and hatred that no appeal has any hope of succeeding.

I thank the Order and my brethren for all their goodness and loyalty and help, especially during these last weeks. I ask pardon for much that was untrue and unjust; and I beg that a little help and care may be given to my aged, sick parents.

The actual reason for my condemnation was that I happened to be, and chose to remain, a Jesuit. There was nothing to show that I had any connection with the attempt on Hitler's life so I was acquitted on that count. The rest of the accusations were far less serious and more factual. There was one underlying theme – a Jesuit is *a priori* an enemy and betrayer of the Reich. So the whole proceedings turned into a sort of comedy developing a theme. It was not justice – it was simply the carrying out of the determination to destroy.

May God shield you all. I ask for your prayers. And I will do my best to catch up, on the other side, with all that I have left undone here on earth.

Towards noon I will celebrate Mass once more and then in God's name take the road under his providence and guidance.

In God's blessing and protection,
Your grateful,
Alfred Delp, S.J.

CPSIA information can be obtained
at www.ICGtesting.com
Printed in the USA
LVHW100137051222
734575LV00003B/406